Isaac Forsyth MacAndrew

On Some Revenue Matters Chiefly in the Province of Oudh

Isaac Forsyth MacAndrew

On Some Revenue Matters Chiefly in the Province of Oudh

ISBN/EAN: 9783337426231

Printed in Europe, USA, Canada, Australia, Japan

Cover: Foto ©ninafisch / pixelio.de

More available books at **www.hansebooks.com**

ON

SOME REVENUE MATTERS

CHIEFLY IN THE

PROVINCE OF OUDH.

BY

LIEUT.-COL. I. F. MACANDREW,
OFFICIATING COMMISSIONER OF SITAPUR.

CALCUTTA:
THACKER, SPINK AND CO.
BOMBAY: THACKER, VINING & CO.   LONDON: W. THACKER & CO.

1876.

PREFACE.

In presenting this little book to the Revenue Officers of Northern India—for it is to them it is addressed rather than to the general public—I wish to say that my object is two-fold : first, to point out a real difference, not generally acknowledged, between the settlement of Oudh and that of the North-Western Provinces ; secondly, to place on record some experience relative to the assessment and collection of the land revenue, which I hope may be of use to those who may be charged with this very important duty in the future.

In endeavouring to carry out the first of these objects I have said nothing of the system of the North-Western Provinces, as it is clearly laid down in the Directions to Revenue Officers, with which I presume the reader to be acquainted ; and I have confined myself to an account of that which in Oudh appears to me to differ, or in the nature of things should differ, from the system in the adjoining larger Government. Matters, therefore, which are not touched upon I consider either are or may be the same in both.

The remarks on assessment and collection are tinged, of course, with the peculiarities of the Oudh revenue system, and I have endeavoured to show where that system entails modifications unnecessary in the North-Western Provinces; but the general drift of my remarks in the chapters referring to these subjects may, I hope, be honoured with some attention beyond the province of Oudh. They are intended for a wider application.

I have to acknowledge the assistance I have received in the collection of the information to be found in these chapters, and especially in that on rent, from the following gentlemen :

Lieut.-Col. CLARK, *Settlement Officer, Kheri.*

Capt. DE MONTMORENCY, *some time Deputy Commissioner of Kheri.*

Mr. H. S. BOYS, C.S., *some time Superintendent, Encumbered Estates.*

Mr. J. HOOPER, C.S., *some time Assistant Commissioner of Sitapur.*

Mr. J. C. WILLIAMS, C.S., *some time Assistant Settlement Officer of Kheri.*

I. F. MACANDREW.

TABLE OF CONTENTS.

	Page.
INTRODUCTION	7
CHAPTER I.—TENURES	15
SECTION 1. Proprietary	15
" 2. Under-proprietary	24
" 3. Perpetual Lease	40
" 4. Farming Lease	41
" 5. Occupancy	42
" 6. Service	45
CHAPTER II.—MUTATIONS	47
" III.—SURFACE, CLIMATE, AND SOILS	51
" IV.—CROPS	57
" V.—RENT	60
SECTION 1. Money Rents	60
" 2. Corn Rents	63
" 3. Mixed Rents	78
CHAPTER VI.—PATWARIS AND THEIR PAPERS	82
" VII.—BOUNDARIES	91
" VIII.—SURVEY	93
" IX.—ASSESSMENT	95
" X.—COLLECTION	121
APPENDIX (FORMS 1 to 5)	131—135

INTRODUCTION.

—:o:—

THE right to the land revenue in Oudh rests on the same basis of the common law of India as it does all over the country. This fundamental principle is affirmed in the preamble to Regulation XXXI of 1803. Nevertheless, in the settlement of the land revenue in Oudh, the Government has departed from the principles which governed that work in the North-Western Provinces, and the deviation in practice has been perhaps still more marked. In Oudh there are to be found tenures of land and customs of rent which, if not peculiar to the province, have nowhere been described by Government authority for the guidance of officers concerned, but which have been recognized by the courts in their decisions, and by the revenue officers in their assessment of the land. The Directions to Revenue Officers is still the text-book for the examination of young officers in the province, though its principles have been so altered by numerous judicial decisions and by the circulars issued under the authority of the Foreign Department letter No. 12, dated 4th February 1856, which received the force of law from the Indian Council's Act of 1861, that the first part of it, the Directions to Settlement Officers, is virtually obsolete. Moreover, the assessment of the land revenue is drawing to a close, and there is now in the province much knowledge and experience regarding that operation which will not be available when the next settlement comes to be made. This knowledge is not always to be found in settlement reports, which, formed perhaps somewhat too exclusively on the old models, deal rather with the relations of the people to the land, which will not have to be determined again, than with the fiscal relations of the people towards the Government which will have to be revised at the end of thirty years.

Now the ancient common law of India declares that the State is entitled to a share of the produce of every acre of land in the country, but it nowhere declares the limit of the Government demand; and immediately previous to our rule, this was a matter of annual bargain between the Government and the people. After two different experiences, in Bengal and Madras, came the settlement of the North-Western Provinces, and the Government, while limiting its demand and fixing it for thirty years, at the same time declared that it had the right to engage, if not with whomsoever it pleased, at least with either party when there were two interests on the land, and as the engagement for the revenue carried with it the right to all the profits left after the payment of the Government demand and such charges as might be imposed by the Government on behalf of third parties, we began to have the phrase "right to engage for the revenue" brought into use.

But in Oudh, those who were found in possession at annexation were declared to be the proprietors, so far as the Government was concerned, and no one was allowed to arraign their title, unless he could show possession within twelve years before annexation. The much-discussed talukdari settlement was formed on this basis, the difference between men declared to be talukdars and other proprietors being this, that no one was allowed to question a talukdar's title on any ground at all. With the proprietors thus authoritatively and judicially declared the engagement for the revenue was made; and hence, in Oudh, the payment of the land revenue became an obligation contingent on a proprietary right in the soil, and not a privilege carrying proprietary rights with it.

This distinction appears to me of vital importance; for the Government of Oudh does not choose the person who becomes liable for the revenue, and is obliged to recognize and maintain all the rights decreed at the settlement, while in the North-West these were declared so as to suit the fiscal arrangements about to be made. It is therefore but reasonable, that in Oudh the proprietor should strictly abide by the settlement; and, in addition to the rule "that the "revenue is always claimable from the person in possession "of the land it is assessed upon," the further rule should be enforced that " the whole of a proprietor's estate is "hypothecated for the revenue on each part of it, and he "cannot transfer his obligation to pay the revenue on any "particular part of it without the consent of the Govern-"ment thereto." The necessity for this becomes very clear when we consider the case of an under-proprietor paying a rent less than the Government revenue on the lands which he holds (a very common case). The superior in this case has generally either acquired a very much larger estate on the condition that he should pay the revenue on the under-proprietary holding, or he has been paid in hard cash or a full equivalent for the right to hold the land at a fixed rent under him, the obligation for the revenue resting on him as before.

It is quite true that the land is liable for the revenue in the last resort; but the tendency of a rule of law is to establish several rights and responsibility in land, and I hold that it is fair and proper, and the logical consequence of our settlement, that we should do all we can to maintain the tenure as it was at annexation, and in such cases as those put, the proprietary right should be sequestrated or be broken up before the under-proprietary right is made liable under the ultimate common law.

This position is, I am afraid, not generally understood even in the province of Oudh; but the joint and several liability of the proprietor and the under-proprietor bears some analogy to the joint and separate liability of a coparcenary community. It is admitted everywhere that, when the lands are distinct and held in severalty, the responsibility of the individual member of the coparcenary community is to be exhausted before the community is made to pay for what is not their fault; and though the Government has never given up its right to hold the whole community responsible in a pattidari estate, the old Regulations were full of the principle of several responsibility, and Act I of 1841 was enacted to give it clearness and precision. This Act has been repealed, but its provisions have been re-enacted in the Local Revenue Acts which have been passed to define the revenue law in the several Governments to which it applied. Nay more, in the Oudh Revenue Bill, in one under-proprietary tenure (sub-settlement), where there is a coparcenary community holding under a talukdar, the separate right of the co-sharers is recognized in conceding to them the right to partition, and there seems to be no reason, either logical or fiscal, why the same essential right should not be conceded to the other under-proprietors, the name of whom, as compared with sub-settlement holders, is legion. This right is, that, having paid their rent if there be any, they should not be held responsible for the revenue for which they did not engage until first all processes of recovery have been exhausted against the proprietor who has engaged to pay it, and who, upon the double condition of paying the revenue and maintaining these under-proprietary rights, has received an indefeasible title to his estate (Schedule I, Act I of 1869).

I am aware that it has been held in some quarters that no under-proprietary right should in any case pay less rent to the proprietor than the Government revenue and cesses. But this principle is not a fact, first, because the law embodied in the schedule above quoted declares that the under-proprietors are to be maintained in the rights they formerly enjoyed, and the proprietors have uniformly refused to increase the under-proprietary holdings, so as to leave the under-proprietors a profit equivalent to that which they are entitled under this law should they be called on to pay rent equal to the Government revenue and cesses. Secondly, because it is the interest of all parties to allow things to remain as they are,—the under-proprietors, because their light rents or no rents protect them from ejectment to a great extent; the proprietor, because it is much easier for him to collect the same rental in lighter rents over a smaller under-proprietary area and in full rents from ordinary tenants over a larger area; than in heavier rents over a larger under-proprietary area; and in full rents from ordinary tenants over a smaller area; and the Government, because whatever makes it easier for the proprietor to recover his rent makes it easier for the Deputy Commissioner to collect the revenue. At the time the earlier instructions for the guidance of Settlement Officers in Oudh were issued, the question of under-proprietary right was not as well understood as it is now. It was then a new question, and it presented many forms and aspects which only experience in working it out could discover, and the notorious facts that the courts found themselves in hundreds of cases obliged to depart from the rule which heads this paragraph and decree under-proprietary tenures at a rent less than the Government revenue, and that lands are now so held under their decrees in every district in Oudh ought to be decisive of this question.

That the settlement would have been more satisfactory had the claimants to talukdari villages been allowed to sue for them, on the basis of the better right under the twelve years law of limitation strictly applied, there is no doubt; but the soil of Oudh was confiscated by conquest, and for political reasons the estates they held at annexation were conferred upon the talukdars, and it is quite too late to question the policy now. But it is not too late to see that, within Lord Canning's settlement, we do justice to all concerned.

Remembering then that the relations of proprietor and under-proprietor are those of persons having a joint and several property in the same land, and that unnecessarily to enforce the joint responsibility for the default of one is to confiscate to that extent the several right of the other, I shall conclude with the following warning which I saw quoted the other day as the recent utterance of Sir Henry Maine: "Nobody is at liberty to attack "several property, and to say, at the same time, that he

INTRODUCTION. 13

" values civilization. The history of the two is insepar-
" able. Civilization is nothing more than a name for the
" new order of the Aryan world dissolved, but perpetually
" reconstituting itself under a vast variety of solvent
" influences, of which indefinitely* the most powerful have
" been those which have slowly, and in some parts of the
" world much less perfectly, substituted several property
" for collective ownership."

---

* Sic in original.

ON
SOME REVENUE MATTERS,
CHIEFLY IN THE
PROVINCE OF OUDH.

—:o:—

CHAPTER I.
TENURES.

Tenures in Oudh may be divided into—

1. Proprietary ... ... *Hak-ála.*
2. Under-proprietary ... ... *Hak Matáhat.*
3. Perpetual Leases ... ... *Patta istamrari.*
4. Farming ditto ... ... *Mustajiri.*
5. Cultivating tenures ... *Hak kashthari.*
6. Service, ditto ... ... *Chakarana.*

Section I.—PROPRIETARY TENURES.

Proprietary tenures may be divided either according to the nature of the property, or according to the relation they may bear to the land revenue. According to the first they are either

1. Talukdari.
2. Single zemindari.
3. Coparcenary.

According to the second they are either

1. Revenue-free ... *Jagir and mafi.*
2. Malikana ... ...
3. Revenue-paying ... ... *Malguzari.*
4. Quit-rent ... ... *Peshkash.*

TALUKDARI TENURE,

In the province of Oudh, has a different signification from what it bears in Bengal or in the North-Western Provinces. It is not necessary in Oudh that there should be superior and a dependent tenure to make the estate a taluka. Under a special Act (I of 1869), every person whose name was entered in a list, prepared by the Chief Commissioner under that Act, became a talukdar. The advantages gained by being enrolled in this golden book of Oudh were, first, an unquestionable title to his property; second, the position of residuary proprietor,—that is, the Government revenue being paid and the profits of under-proprietors and other claimants to beneficial interest being fixed, all the rest, including the increased value of the property arising from the security of British rule, belongs to the talukdar; third, a special law of succession, gift, and bequest laid down in the Act already mentioned. The conditions upon which the talukdars hold their estates are—

1st.—Loyalty to the British Government.

2nd.—Payment of the Government revenue assessed upon their estates.

3rd.—The maintenance of those holding under them in the rights they formerly enjoyed.

SINGLE ZEMINDARI TENURE.

This is the proprietorship of a single person, and is held under the general guarantee and obligations of the law; lands held by single proprietors who are not talukdars being classed under this head. Their title is not protected by any special legislation, though it has been the custom in Oudh, in estates where there is a superior and inferior

CHAP. I.]   COPARCENARY TENURES.   17

right, always to look on the superior as the residuary proprietor, and therefore to take the engagement for the Government revenue from him. As regards succession, bequest, or gift, these tenures follow the law or custom of the caste, tribe, or religion to which the proprietor may belong.

COPARCENARY TENURES.

These are usually divided into three main classes—
1. Zemindari.
2. Pattidari.
3. Bhayachara.

Zemindari is where an estate is held in common, the Government revenue and other liabilities are first paid out of the rents, and the remainder is divided among the coparceners, according to their recorded shares. Sometimes the coparcenary is an undivided Hindu family. In such case there is no division, but all get maintenance, and the family extraordinary expenses are paid from the common fund administered by its head.

Pattidari is where all the land in an estate is divided, and each pattidar holds his share separately. The individual liabilities of the pattidars are regulated by their respective shares as recorded, not as actually held. It is not the custom in Oudh to re-arrange the liabilities to make them correspond with the holdings, or to redistribute the lands to make them correspond with the shares. Native officers often try to do this in cases of partition, but it is contrary both to the customs of the people and the instructions given for the settlement. The true principle is to maintain the status existing throughout the term of limitation should it have existed so long.

Imperfect pattidari is where some of the lands are held in severalty and some in common, and the rents of the common lands go first towards the revenue and the other liabilities. Should there be any surplus, it is divided in proportion to the recorded shares; should there be a deficit, it is made up by a proportional contribution from co-sharers.

Bhyachara is where all the land comprising the estate is divided and is held in severalty, the liabilities of the co-sharers being assessed on the holdings. Though generally the assessment is levied on the holdings, it is not always so done; for instance, it is sometimes levied on the homesteads, sometimes on the ploughs, and it may be levied in any way agreed upon.

Imperfect bhyachara is where part of the land is held in severalty in bhyachara tenure, and part in common. In such tenures there is always a special village custom for determining the liabilities of the common land, and the rights of the co-sharers therein.

But it would be a great mistake to suppose that these definitions will explain the constitution of the various coparcenary communities existing in the province, or even of the majority of them. It will more frequently happen that the constitution of the coparcenary may answer to none of these definitions, but rather partake of one or more of them. Not only will it be found that in some cases the component thoks and pattis have internally different constitutions, but the direct constitution of a thok or patti may embrace more than one of these principles. It is common for an estate to be undivided except the sír; but it is also common for the sír to bear no relation whatever to the share either in area or value, and also for one co-sharer to pay a different rate of rent from another on his sír lands without reference to the quality of the soil. An estate of this kind has been usually classed at settlement as zemindari, though it is manifestly either pattidari or bhyachara so far as the sír lands are concerned. Mortgages with special conditions attached will also be found greatly to alter the former nature of tenures, as, for example, the biswi mortgages of Fajzabad and Sultanpur. Infinite varieties of tenure will be found to result from the operation of these and other causes, which may have their origin in the superior influence or industry of the individual coparcener, or in his extravagance, carelessness, pious alienations of his lands, or passion for planting groves. It would be unjust to tie down a property for all time to the strict definition of the Directions under such circumstances, and no Civil Court will do so with evidence of possession and the statute of limitation before it.

Hence the great importance of ascertaining the real nature of the coparcenary tenure in an estate before making any of those arrangements for it which the revenue officer is occasionally called upon to make, such as those incident to partition, to the transfer of a patti, or to cancelment of settlement whether prior to direct management or to farm.

It was intended that all this should be made clear in the administration paper, and that this document should promptly explain the constitution of the village. But not only do these things alter and administration papers become obsolete, but there is reason to fear that this paper has not always been prepared with care and impartiality, and that in many cases it is anything but a trustworthy guide. It can only be held to bind those who have signed it, and then it should have a presumption in its favor, and the onus of proving it wrong should rest with those who question it. But in any of the important cases above referred to its provisions should be explained to the coparceners, and they should be asked if it really represents the constitution of the village at that then present time, and the revenue officer should proceed no further until this point has been cleared up. It cannot be too strongly impressed upon every revenue officer that, before he passes any orders which alter the relations of the coparceners in an estate to Government, their landlord, or each other, he should accurately inform himself concerning those relations, and have a careful regard to them in any necessary interference.

Revenue Free.

At the time of the settlement of the province claims to hold land revenue-free were investigated, it being one of the principles laid down in the preamble to Regulation XXXI of 1803, that no land can be exempt from its liability to Government revenue unless such exemption has been sanctioned by the Government itself. The Government of India alone, therefore, has now power to declare land exempt from revenue demand. At the settlement, however, the claims were decided on the following principle. If the sanad of the British Government, or the Padshah of Delhi, or the Nawab of Oudh could be shown, the revenue was released in perpetuity. If not, possession for three generations, or twenty years, gave a title to release for the life of the then incumbent. The revenue of lands set apart for religious or charitable endowments was released for so long as the said institutions are kept up. The revenue of lands held free, by way of pension for service done, was released for the life of the person in possession. In special cases, with the sanction of Government, the revenue of lands might be released for one or more lives. All other revenue-free lands were resumed either at once or at the regular settlement. Revenue-free lands are known as *jagir* and *máfi*. The jagir is generally a comparatively large estate, the máfi a comparatively small one. The difference between them is this. In máfi the presumption is that the máfidar is the proprietor, and on the resumption of the máfi, any one who asails his title has to prove his right. In jagir the presumption is that the proprietary right does not belong to the jagirdar, and the onus lies on him to prove his right in case of resumption. The revenue officer in such case would take engagements from the actual occupants, unless the jagirdar made out a case to his satisfaction. Jagir is sometimes used to describe rent-free village service tenures. The word is not so used here at all. Such tenures are described under the head of chakarana. Revenue-free lands are all liable for the cesses, and to determine them they were assessed at the settlement. When resumed, the proprietor is entitled to hold them at the revenue assessed upon them at the time of the current settlement for the period it has to run.

MALIKANA.

Malikána is of three kinds:—First, when there is a superior and an inferior right in the same estate, and the Government under Regulation VII of 1822 sets aside the superior and engages direct for the revenue with the inferior, an allowance of not less than ten per cent. on the revenue assessed is made to the superior, and is called malikána. Secondly, when Government cancels a settlement for arrears of revenue, preparatory to assuming direct management or farming it to a stranger, the law provides that the ejected proprietor shall receive a malikána which shall not be less than five per cent. on the revenue assessed. In both the above cases the malikána is the first charge on the rental, and has priority of the revenue itself; the reason being that this dispossession is the act of the Government for its own convenience. Thirdly, in some cases the proprietor of an estate has voluntarily made over the management to another person on condition of receiving a certain fixed sum as malikána. These tenures have been respected and upheld by our Courts, and decrees have been given for them. This description of malikána, however, is a claim on the rental next after the Government revenue only, and this because the Government was not a party to the transaction. It is nevertheless a proprietary and not an under-proprietary right, for the málik is the superior of the malguzar, and his position is to receive malikána from the malguzar, not to hold land under him and pay rent.

Revenue Paying Tenures.

Malguzari estates are held on the condition of payment of the Government revenue assessed upon them. The law is that, whatever arrangements may be made by the parties having interests in the land, the ultimate lien of the Government on the land is never lost; and if the revenue is not paid, the Government, should it think necessary, may suspend the exercise of all beneficiary rights, or even sweep them entirely away, by the sale of the tenure free of all incumbrances not recorded at settlement, in order to satisfy the revenue demand. Nevertheless, so long as the revenue demand is satisfied, it is not the policy of the Government to interfere in any way with the exercise of the right of property belonging to the individual. The whole of the estate for which a proprietor gives a kabuliat is hypothecated for the revenue assessed on each part of it so long as that settlement lasts, and the sale or mortgage of a part of it during the currency of the settlement does not relieve the vendor or the mortgagor or his remaining estate from liability for the revenue on the portion sold or mortgaged; though, as the Government never loses its lien on the land itself, the sale or mortgage creates a right of demand on the part of the Government against the vendee or mortgagee. The process by which the liability is transferred with the consent of the Government is termed mutation, or *dákhil khárij*; and under that heading, I shall have a caution to address to officers having to deal with such applications, which are in my opinion far too lightly sanctioned.

QUIT-RENT.

There appears, from the Financial Commissioner's Circular No. 28 of 1869, to have been in the Faizabad district certain grants, originally revenue-free under the sanads of the Padshahs of Delhi or the Nawabs of Oudh, upon which the Oudh officials had levied a '*peshkash*' for their own benefit. Saadat Ali Khan, in his celebrated settlement of 1814, maintained these grants as they were, but swept the 'peshkash' into the royal treasury. At the investigation into revenue-free tenures some of these grants were maintained at the quit-rent for ever. They therefore form a separate class of proprietary tenures. I think also that the estate given to the Rajah of Kapurthalla for his conduct during the mutiny war, and the hereditary estates of the five loyal talukdars mentioned in the second Schedule to Act I of 1869, though talukas, come under this category, for these estates are assessed on exceptionally favorable terms and the revenue-demand thus fixed is perpetual.

Section II.—UNDER-PROPRIETARY TENURES.

Under-proprietary right, though by no means peculiar to Oudh, has been recognized and defined in this province with a precision that is not to be found elsewhere. In the North-West, the class whom we term under-proprietors were either admitted to direct engagements with the State, their superior being set aside by the process described under malikána, or they were recorded as cultivators with an heritable and non-transferable title at a rent fixed for the term of the settlement. The passing of Act X of 1859, however, made these rents liable to enhancement, and Act XVIII of 1873 has not altered their status in this respect except by defining more strictly the possible occasions of enhancement. In Oudh, these tenures have been decreed by the courts either rent-free, at a rent fixed in perpetuity, or at a rent proportional to the Government revenue : they are heritable and transferable.

The great difference between proprietary and under-proprietary tenures is this : while the right of a proprietor in a malguzari estate depends on the discharge of his obligation towards the Government alone, that of an under-proprietor depends not only on the discharge of his obligation to pay rent to his superior, if such be an incident of his tenure which it generally is, but also on the discharge by the superior of his obligation to pay the Government revenue ; for, in the last resort, the under-proprietary tenure is liable for the revenue whether the incumbent has paid his rent or not. The essential feature of an under-proprietary tenure is that it is a tenure dependent on another tenure.

The better known under-proprietary tenures in Oudh bear the following names :—

1 Sub-Settlement.
2 Dídarí.
3 Sír.
4 Naukár.
5 Purwa bassána.
6 Birt.
7 Shankalp.
8 Dár.
9 Marwat.
10 Daswant.
11 Biswi.

The two first tenures are always founded upon former full proprietary right, and Nos. 3 and 4 generally so, though sometimes these names are applied to the interest of the under-proprietors in tenures Nos. 5 and 10. From No. 5 onwards, the rights are created by the superior proprietor, and in all cases, except true shankalp, which is a religious grant for value received in some shape or other. This will be apparent when we come to see what was the origin of these several tenures. The fact is worthy of note here, however, as showing on what a sound basis the native polity in the matter of land tenures is founded. I have observed, in the course of my own experience, that where the under-tenure was based on former proprietary right, there was generally no sanad or patta for it, and, if there was a patta, it was given to mark a new arrangement about the rent, and not as an acknowledgment of former proprietary right. Such a document in the Nawabi would have been scorned. But in the case of a tenure given by the proprietor, a written title was added, though it might not always be forthcoming.

4

Sub-Settlement

Is a tenure created by us, for it did not exist under native rule. It is the residuary proprietary right in a village, hamlet, or chak, subject to a rent proportional to the Government revenue. The proportion is not invariable. It was established as the nearest thing which would combine the certainty of a tenure under English rule with the status of a former proprietor leasing a village under a talukdar. But under native rule, the people, in whose favor this tenure has been erected, had no right to a lease of the village. The settlements of the Government with the proprietors, and of the talukdars with the under-proprietors, were annual, and if they could not come to terms, the superior ejected the inferior and assumed direct management. If this was done amicably and peaceably, the person ejected, whether proprietor or under-proprietor, enjoyed certain lands for his maintenance either rent-free or at a peppercorn rent, which lands were known by the name of sír or nankár. Under such a Government as that of the Nawabi every institution in the country was modified by force, and we find cases, especially in Eastern Oudh, where the under-proprietors had completely the upper hand, and the talukdar was nothing but *primus inter pares*, a mere representative of the common dignity. But, as a rule, the force was on the side of the talukdar, and he had acquired an ascendancy, even over those under-proprietors whose estates had come into his taluka, which made them, as far as the lease was concerned, the creatures of his will; and their going into court to acquire a right, which would reduce him to the position of a person entitled to a quit-rent, but excluded from all personal management of and interference with the village, became a measure which the talukdars resented with all the means in their power. The idea of the talukdars was that the under-proprietors were to get what they held in the Nawabi and nothing more: their contention was that the under-proprietors had never held such a right as sub-settlement, which was certainly true, and they bitterly resented this invasion of their rights guaranteed by Her Majesty's Government. There can be no doubt that the rights of an under-proprietor, in talukas generally under native rule, was measured by the amount of beneficial interest he enjoyed when dispossessed of the village.

Had we been content to record this sír and nankár as an under-proprietary right, and to leave the lease an open question, we should have acted much more wisely than we have done; for, as it is, the sub-settlement holders are fairly on the road to ruin. The sale of their rights is a mere question of time, and when the sale does come, the most that can be retained for them, will be a right of occupancy in their sír lands, instead of a full under-proprietary right therein with the rent fixed for the term of a settlement at a proportion to the Government revenue assessed upon the land.

But we did not do so. The proceedings of the Courts became so hostile to the talukdars, that they appealed to the Government, and Act XXVI of 1866 was passed. Its failure is notorious as a practical measure; for while the holders of sub-settlements are gradually going to the wall, the landlord does not get his rent, nor the Government its revenue.

The position, that sub-settlements or anything really resembling them existed in the Nawabi, being abandoned, the contention of the advocates of the tenure amounts to this. If it be true, as I assert it is, that, under native rule, neither proprietors nor under-proprietors had any right to engage for or manage the village, but that the superior could always collect the rents directly if he pleased and was strong enough; then, "if we give the proprietor a "perpetual title instead of the lease we found him in "possession of, and fix his payments for thirty years, it is "but fair to do the same for the under-proprietor also. "One class of Her Majesty's subjects should not alone "benefit from her rule." To this there is a two-fold answer: first, we may not, because Lord Canning's settlement barred the creation in talukas, without the consent of the talukdar, of any under-proprietary or occupancy tenure not then existing; and, while sub-settlement is a tenure of the former kind, the estates in which they are claimed are nearly always talukas; secondly, we ought not, because, though it was expedient to create the proprietary right of the man who paid revenue to the State, it was not expedient to create a new under-proprietary right in the shape of a sub-settlement in favor of the man who paid rent to a private person. The first of these positions will be generally admitted; on the second it is necessary to say a few words.

Experience has clearly shown that, where a village has been sub-settled, the under-proprietors do not, as a general rule, get on with the talukdar, and unless they are very good managers, or hold the village on unusually favorable terms, they can hardly avoid falling into the talukdar's debt in a bad season; for the case mentioned in para. 9 of the Schedule to Act XXVI of 1866 is the ordinary one, in which the liabilities of the sub-settlement holders are 85 per cent. of the gross rental, for they have to pay the chaukidar, the patwári, and the village expenses, amounting to not less than ten per cent. of the gross rental of the village, in addition to the 75 per cent. laid down in the paragraph quoted.

In such a case, as the sub-settlement holders are ordinarily a coparcenary body without capital or with very little, it is not the interest of the talukdar to press them hard at first. The law allows him three years wherein to bring a suit for arrears and three years more wherein to execute it, and if this is properly worked by a man anxious above everything to destroy the tenure, it becomes almost impossible for the Court ultimately to refuse sanction to its sale, and then who in such a position to buy it as the talukdar?

Didári.

Didári is a certain amount of land rent-free, and has always, I believe, its origin in former proprietorship. When pressed by the Názims under the later native rule, the proprietors often found they could not get on, and voluntarily sought the protection of some neighbouring talukdar, who then took the management of the estate and whatever profit he could get out of it, and the smaller and former proprietor took a piece of land varying according to the property he made over. This was rent-free for ever, as the rest of the estate was chargeable with the revenue upon this portion, and in Eastern Oudh the tenure is called didári. It is more commonly known by that name in Faizabad, Sultanpur, and Gonda. A consideration of the conditions of this tenure shows how necessary it is in Oudh to hold by the principle that no man can relieve himself of his obligation to pay the revenue without the consent of Government except by the surrender of his whole estate. If he could do so in a case like this, he could confiscate one-half of the tenure the maintenance of which is the condition on which he holds his estate under his sanad, and Lord Canning's letters of the 10th and 19th October 1859 made unquestionable law by Act I of 1869. It is manifestly unjust to apply strictly the principle that the holder of the land must pay the revenue assessed upon it, where under-proprietary tenures prevail.

Sír.

Sír, as found and decreed in Oudh, is an under-proprietary right, and has its origin both in former proprietorship and in the act of the superior proprietor. It is also the term applied to the land held in cultivating occupancy by a proprietor. If it is cultivated by the hands of the proprietor or by his hired servants using his bullocks and ploughs, it is called *khudkásht* or *nijjot*, if it is let to a tenant, such tenant is termed *shikmi*, not *assámi*, the name applied to tenants generally. These terms are also used with respect to the sír of an under-proprietor. Sír, so far as I know, always pays rent, but it is a low one. Whenever I have found sír rent-free, part of the released rent was a nankár deduction. Sír is emphatically what a proprietor or under-proprietor was allowed to hold for his own subsistence when he did not hold the lease of the village or estate. In coparcenary communities, whether proprietary or under-proprietary, the sír frequently bears no proportion or relation to the shares, and though the law of the North-Western Provinces, as laid down in the Directions and Regulation VII of 1822, permitted the re-adjustment of these sír holdings so as to bring them into harmony with the shares, it has never been the practice in Oudh, where the maintenance of the separate possession within the term of limitation has been the sheet anchor of the settlement of the province. The law which permitted the contrary practice (Clause 2, Section XII, Regulation VII of 1822) has now been repealed by Act XVI of 1874. The safe rule is always to maintain the possession in severalty, by whatever name it may be called, which has lasted throughout the term of limitation. If the possession in severalty has not lasted so long, the administration paper should be consulted, and if the disputants were consenting parties to that document, they would be bound by its provisions. In addition to the provisions of the Government letters of the 10th and 19th October 1859, which provide for the maintenance of all rights held under talukdars at the annexation of the province or within what has been fixed as the limitation, which letters are law under Act I of 1869, sír is one of those under-proprietary rights for the maintenance of which, when its origin is former proprietorship, there is a special law (Clause 10, Schedule to Act XXVI of 1866).

NANKAR.

Nankár was originally a deduction from the revenue of a village or estate allowed by the Government for managing it. In the time of Akbar Padshah, his dewan, Todar Mal, made a regular assessment of the whole empire founded on an estimate of the produce, and he fixed a certain portion of it as the demand of the State; but when the Moghal Empire went to pieces, the Mahomedan princes who succeeded were not satisfied with this. They claimed the whole *kacha nikasi*, and allowed a deduction, which was called nankár. The kacha nikasi was not the gross rental of the village, but the rental as entered in the jamabandi. Thus the sír lands were not entered at their real value, but at the peppercorn rent at which they were held when the proprietors did not engage for the village, and all the other lands held at favored (*riayatti*) rents in the same way. The people thus had a large share of the profits when the villages were held direct, and they would have required it for the nankár was very small. There is extant a genuine copy of Nawab Saadat Ali Khan's assessment of the parganah of Bareli, and the jama is Rs. 1,92,430, while the nankár is only Rs. 4,522. It is plainly impossible that those holding proprietary rights of all kinds in this parganah could have existed on so small a share of the profits. In talukas nankár generally took the shape of some revenue-free villages, but in single villages it was usually a cash deduction from the revenue. As nankár was small, it was not unfrequently retained by former proprietor on the incorporation of his village with the taluka, and becoming then a deduction from the rent of his sír lands, those lands, or a portion of them, sometimes appear rent-free, and the fact of the under-proprietor enjoying nankár at all is apt to be lost sight of. The name of nankár is also sometimes applied to a right in land created by a talukdar in favor of men who founded hamlets and settled cultivators on lands either waste, or hitherto cultivated without irrigation or manure by non-resident cultivators. In such case it is a right conceded in return for the increased rental, which the talukdar received in consequence of the settlement. There are other kinds of nankár, known as *ismi* and *tankhai*, in the province, but they come rather under the category of revenue-free holdings, they have all been long ago finally disposed of, and were certainly not under-proprietary rights.

Purwa Bassána.

This is the first of the tenures created by a superior in favor of a man in lieu of value received. Purwas are known by other names, such as *khera*, *mazra*, or *dákhili*. They are hamlets founded on certain lands in a larger village or mauzah, and they have not a separate number and hadbast character of their own. The land on which they are founded is either waste or cultivated in an inferior manner, and they are usually settled by persons with some influence among the cultivators they bring, and with sufficient capital to make them the necessary advances. It was common, under the native system, for the superior in such cases to lease the lands forming the purwa to the founder, and in case he would not take it on the terms offered in any year, he was secured his under-proprietary right of sír or nankár or both, as is shown by the following copy of a sanad for a purwa in Rai Bareli :—

"Sanad granted by Thákar Rámdin to Jowáhir to the "following effect :—Do you found a katra after the name of "Bhagwán Bakhsh in Mauzah Deopur, and populate it, build "your own house therein, and be assured that I have written "off the zemindari of the same to you. Whoever comes "and settles in it, do you remit his forced labour (begár). "So long as you wish you may hold *pakka* (lease of the "village), and when it is made *kacha* (direct collection "from the cultivators) you may enjoy 10 bigahs nankár, "and 15 bigahs sír, assessed at one rupee eight annas,

"and in addition take 10 bigahs *charri* (grazing land).
"Dated Kuár Badi Panchmi Sambat 1901 (1252 Fasli)."

Signed by Debidin Mutsadi.

"Who says the sanad is correct.

"Further 3 bigahs are given you for a grove that you may rest quiet in your mind."

Detail of Sir.

Name of Field.	Area.	
	Bigahs.	Biswas.
Mati	3	0
Mati, 2nd	2	10
Gurhas	2	10
Beyas	2	10
Manic	3	10
Massi	1	0
Total	15	0

Detail of Nunkar.

	Bigahs.	Biswas.
Aintha	4	0
Naitha	3	0
Mati	1	10
Mati, 2nd	1	10
Total	10	0

This shows very clearly the nature of the under-proprietary tenures, the object of which was land improvement. The talukdar in return for his concession obtained a great increase to the rental of his estate, and the sanad clearly provides for the interest of the purwa founder in case they cannot come to terms about the rent. A consideration of the terms of this sanad, which really describes the ordinary nature of under-proprietary right under whatever name it may be known, will show what an interference with the constitution of that village it would be to decree the purwa founder a sub-settlement. If a man cannot see that, he is incapable of taking an impartial view of anything. This tenure, besides being an under-proprietary right by the Government letters in the 1st Schedule to Act I of 1869, is specially protected by para. 11 of the Schedule to Act XXVI of 1866.

BIRT.

Birt prevails chiefly in the districts of Gondah, Baraich and Faizabad. It is an under-proprietary right created by a talukdar in return for money paid. Rent was paid for it, but it was a low rent, and the rent was understood to be fixed, though no doubt it was raised sometimes by the pressure of the talukdar. Still it is always found at a rent favorable as compared with non-proprietary holdings. Another kind of birt is described in the Oudh record of rights Circular, No. 2 of 1861, as having its origin in a lease for clearing jungle land. This is *daswant* under another name, and will be described under that heading. The following is a copy of a birt patta :—

"Birt patta dated Sáwan Sudhi 8th 1238 Fasli. Patta "written by Rájah Shri Kishn Parshád Singh. I have "given Tulsi Rám Misr a birt. He is to get (continuously) "mauzah Garmeapur, tank, groves, dih, parjah, anjuri, biswa, "bondha. He is to get (continuously) the zemindari hak, "whether the village be pakka or kacha. He is to take "possession in confidence. Rupees 701 have been taken. "Witness Banki Singh Sangam Misr. Written by Bháwani "Baksh Mutsaddi. N. B.—On the top is the sign manual "of the Rájah."

This is by no means such a precise document as the one quoted for the purwa, for though it states that the birtea is to have the zemindari hak when out of managing possession it does not detail what that right is. It is however precisely of the same nature, and it shows that the tenure is really a partial sale of the proprietary right.

SHANKALP.

Shankalp is in some parts much the same as birt, an under-proprietary right bought with money, but true shankalp is a rent-free religious gift known as *bishnprit* (for the love of God) or *kushast* (from kusha the sacred grass of the Hindus, which was given unto the hand of the Brahmin). In the Oudh record of rights Circular, No. 2 of 1861, para. 26, it is stated that the bought shankalp can be redeemed at any time by the grantor on payment of the original purchase-money. I exceedingly doubt this. It is manifestly unjust, for these holdings, as a rule, were greatly improved, the original grant being generally poorly cultivated land, and this would be still more conspicuous when the tenure come under English rule. I think that the fact that any arrangement is unjust raises a strong presumption against its being a genuine Hindu custom regarding landed property, and the tendency of Hindu polity is to stereotype arrangement of this kind once made. These bought shankalps are only found where birt prevails, and I think they were birts made to Brahmins who called them shankalps, because greater sanctity attached to that name, and the tenures were less likely to be interfered with by violence. Their being found in the Faizabad district in the hands of Chamárs may be accounted for by their sale, as there would be no sanctity in the eyes of their original Brahmin holders which should prevent it. The religious shankalp, so far as I know, was one of the most respected of under-proprietary rights. The primary meaning of the word shankalp is vow, and its secondary meaning is alms. The gift was usually made on occasions of sorrow and rejoicing, such as bereavement, marriage, or the birth of a son. It was only made to a Brahmin. It was heritable, and was freely mortgaged. It was never resumed, and it was considered unlucky for one to lapse for want of heirs. It is the only under-proprietary right of which I have knowledge that no equivalent has been given for, unless the prayers and blessings of the Brahmin be considered one. It has been decreed at the settlement as an under-proprietary right, and is generally small and rent-free.

DÁR.

This tenure is confined I believe to the parganah of Patti Dalippur in the Pratábgarh district, and is similar to birt. It is a purchased tenure in a patch of land or chak, and is obtainable by all classes. It is never found to extend to entire villages. The real and primary meaning of the word dár is obscure, but it is said to be a corruption of zemindari. The extent of this tenure is very trifling, said to be only 403 acres, and it is mentioned here solely to show that under-proprietary rights may here and there exist under local names which would escape general observation, and that the real test of them is their origin combined with the existence of a present decided beneficiary interest.

MARWAT.

Marwat is an under-proprietary right, granted to the family of a man slain in battle for the talukdar. It generally pays a low rent, and is never resumed. No doubt some two generations or so afterwards the talukdar himself, pressed by the Nazim, might raise the marwatti's rent, but it would be still a low one easy to be distinguished from the assámiwar holdings. I have known a whole village held on a marwat tenure, but, as a rule, the holdings are small.

DASWANT.

Daswant is an under-proprietary right derived from a jungle-clearing lease (*bankatta*), and the term is in use chiefly in Gondah and Baraich. The terms of the lease were usually as follows:—For five years the land was rent-free; in the sixth year, the tenant paid one-sixth of the produce; in the seventh, one-fifth; in the eighth, one-fourth; in the ninth, one-third; and in the tenth, one-half, the full rent. Henceforward the clearer was entitled to hold at that rent so long as the land was pakka; but if the landlord held kacha, the clearer was entitled to have one-tenth of the produce, which in practice came to mean one-tenth of the land rent-free, in under-proprietary right. This tenure, like the others, was liable to encroachment in the shape of an assessment of rent, but that would be low in any case. The tenure is however known in other districts by such names as birt, sír, and nankár. I take the law on this subject to be that, if the person claiming an under-proprietary right based on a clearing of the jungle could show that he or his ancestors really had cleared the land, and that he held it at a favored (*riáyatti*) rent, the presumption was that he held an under-proprietary right; but if his rent was an ordinary one, the presumption was against him; and if he could get anything in consideration of the clearing, in the absence of positive contract, it could be only under Section 22 of the Rent Act.

Biswi.

Biswi is a mortgage by a proprietor to a cultivator of the latter's holding for a sum of money paid down. Generally a low rent was reserved, and this rent was called *parmsána*; which is the difference between the full rent and the interest on the money. The parmsána was not unfrequently less than the Government jama for which the mortgagor was liable. Sometimes the biswi was rent-free. Naturally, with such an origin, these tenures were very small, and having been created by coparceners with but small shares, they became very troublesome, as it was not possible to collect the revenue from the zemindars when their rents were gone. It is this consideration which places the tenure under the class of under-proprietary rights. It is a tenure dependent on another tenure; and the settlement having been made with the zemindars there is nothing else for it, though it differs from all other under-proprietary rights in being liable to redemption. But I am of opinion that a mistake was made at the settlement in regard of these tenures. It would have been far better to have treated them as simple mortgages, and where the zemindars were insolvent or likely to become so, to have applied Section 10, Regulation VII of 1822, and taken the engagement for the Government revenue direct from the biswidars. I believe this tenure is confined to Faizabad and Sultanpur.

In all these tenures it will be observed that the Government revenue is payable by the superior. The under-proprietor pays rent recoverable under the Rent Act.

Section III.—PERPETUAL LEASES.

These tenures are a creation of the Oudh Administration. They were supposed to be the result of agreements registered under Section 326 or 327 of Act VIII of 1859 I believe, but at any rate judicial decrees were given for them, and they stand on that foundation now. They were intended as a compromise in cases where a claim to sub-settlement was not made out, and they differ in two particulars from that tenure: 1st.—Though heritable they are not transferable; 2nd.—The rent is not fixed on any principle, but arbitrarily at the pleasure of the Court. I have seen a case in which the rent, after being once fixed, has been subsequently twice raised on the petition of the talukdar. The creation of this tenure was a great administrative mistake, and shows how inferior is the work of amateurs to the spontaneous growth resulting from the necessities of the people. Difficulties very soon arose. Some of these perpetual lessees fell into arrears of rent, and their landlords, having got decrees against them, claimed to eject them at the end of fifteen days under Section 41 of the Rent Act. Of course this would have defeated the whole object of the creation of the tenure, and the Judicial Commissioner ruled that they were not tenants under the Rent Act. This erected them into *quasi* under-proprietors. But when an under-proprietor falls into arrears of rent, the only way in which at present a decree for the arrears can be executed, is to proceed against the tenure, and these perpetual leases were not transferable. The Chief Commissioner, however, has ruled that they can be held in sequestration, or sold in execution of a decree for rent. The present position of these perpetual lessees would therefore seem to be that of under-proprietors without the right of private transfer. There is no doubt that their existence is dependent on the discharge of his obligations to the State by the talukdar.

Section IV.—FARMING LEASES.

Farming leases appear to me to be of three kinds: *First:*—When an estate is sold for arrears of revenue, and no one will bid on account of over-assessment, the Deputy Commissioner is obliged to buy in the estate on behalf of Government and let it to a farmer for what it will fetch. This tenure, common in Bengal, where the rigidity of the settlement law prevents re-assessment of the estate, is practically unknown, and should remain so in Oudh, because the Government will always permit a revision of the assessment upon proper cause being shown. *Second:*—When an estate is in arrears of revenue, and it has been determined to cancel the settlement and farm the estate for a term of years, or when an under-proprietary estate has against it an unsatisfied decree for rent, and the management having been made over to the Deputy Commissioner under Section 125 of the Rent Act, that officer determines upon sequestration, it is carried out under the provisions of Section 4, Regulation IX of 1825. In this case the position of the farmer as regards the state is as follows: His tenure is neither heritable nor transferable by his private act, and it is determined by his death or if he falls into arrears, in which case the lease may be disposed of and the arrears recovered in the manner provided in Section 18, Regulation XXVII of 1803. *Third:*—When, in the execution of a civil decree, the court farms an estate under Section 243, or the Deputy Commissioner does so under Section 244 of

Act VIII of 1859; or when, in the execution of a decree for rent in an under-proprietary estate, the court, under Section 125 of the Rent Act, itself exercises the power given to it under Section 243 of Act VIII of 1859, and leases the land to a stranger; or when a private person farms a portion of his estate to one who is not a cultivator, the farmer is in the position of a tenant with a lease only, and can be ejected or proceeded against for arrears of rent under the provisions of the Rent Act alone. In all the above cases, the farmer, as respects those below him, is a landlord, and entitled to all the rights of one under the Rent Act.

Section V.—CULTIVATING TENURES.

Cultivating tenures are of two kinds :—*first*, with a right of occupancy; *secondly*, at will.

Occupancy Tenures.

There are four kinds of occupancy tenures in Oudh. *First :*—Those which may have been decreed by a Civil Court. Under Lord Canning's settlement, finally declared by Act I of 1869, all holding under the talukdars were to be maintained in the rights they heretofore enjoyed; and though it has been decided after enquiry, and has been affirmed by the courts, that mere prescription does not create a right of occupancy in Oudh, yet this by no means declares that such a tenure may not exist founded on some actual contract or legal recognition. In the Foreign Department letter No. 302, dated 6th October 1864, Lord Lawrence laid it down that "no declaration of the non-existence of cultivating rights is of any validity," and he directed that all such claims were to be "investigated and tried on their merits." Under these instructions, claims have been heard and in some instances decreed, and I presume that, as a rule, the decree specifies the rent which the tenant has to pay: should the court have omitted to do so, the rent would naturally be fixed under the provisions of the Rent Act. *Secondly :*—There is the tenure decreed under Section 5 of the Rent Act, the nature of which is fully defined in the Act. *Thirdly :*—There is the right of occupancy in their sír lands similar to that of the Rent Act, reserved by the Judicial Commissioner in favor of judgment-debtors whose estates have been sold in execution of decrees of court. *Fourthly :*—By the Chief Commissioner's Revenue Circular, 16 of 1874, in villages given by Government to persons without a legal right to them, a right of occupancy, at rents fixed for the term of the settlement, has been created in favor of residents in the village who have cultivated therein since the re-occupation of the province in 1858, and at rents fixed for five years in favor of tenants resident in the village who are not of such long standing. It may be observed that, though the tenure in the first class may, and in the fourth class does, differ from the second and third in the matter of the rent reserved to the landlord, yet in all four classes the tenure is held on condition of payment of the rent fixed upon it, and, if such rent is not paid, the tenant is liable to ejectment under the provisions of Section 41 of the Rent Act.

On the promulgation of Circular 16 of 1874, a question arose whether such a right could be recorded in favor of persons paying corn rents. It was contended that, as the rent in such case was entirely dependent on the cultivation, if the landlord's power of ejectment was taken away, there was no security whatever for the cultivation of the land, or if to avoid this the condition of cultivation was made an incident of the tenure, for the adequate cultivation of the land. After some correspondence it became evident that a money rent was a necessary condition of a right of occupancy, and it was ordered that when the tenant was holding at a corn rent and refused to commute it into a cash rent, the rent was to be fixed in cash and put into the patta, and the tenant can commute at any time by giving three months' notice before the end of the Fasli year. Should the tenant not cultivate with due diligence, the landlord may apply to the Collector, who, if satisfied that the husbandry has been bad, will be authorized to compel the tenant to commute or to vacate the land.

TENURES-AT-WILL.

Tenants-at-will cannot hold against the will of the landlord, provided the latter proceeds against them as laid down in the Rent Act. The landlord cannot raise their rent without their consent, but he can eject them by a notice to quit at the proper season of the year. It is competent to the tenant to contest such notice by a suit within a given time on the grounds laid down in Section 37 of the Rent Act, or that he has not been compensated for improvements in manner provided in Sections 22 to 26 of the Act, and the courts are directed, by Rent Act Ruling II, to accept a *primâ facie* case of right as sufficient to cancel the notice and uphold the possession of the tenant, throwing on the landlord the onus of bringing a suit to declare what the tenant's right may be.

Section VI.—SERVICE TENURES.

Under the Native Government, there were several hereditary officers who were paid by assignments of land revenue-free. Of these the only one now remaining is the kanungo, and his office is not so distinctly hereditary as it was, for the orders in respect of this officer exact qualifications which I am afraid but few possess. The cases in which the kanungos are still paid in revenue-free lands have all been disposed of, and cannot come before revenue officers except for resumption. All newly-appointed kanungos are paid in cash, a mode of payment which gives the district officer far more authority and control. In the village communities, it is customary to pay the carpenter, the blacksmith, the washerman, the priest, &c., with assignments of land rent-free or at a low rent, in addition to the small quantity of grain each assámi gives them in recompense for their services. These persons, however, can be looked upon as nothing but tenants at the will of zemindars: there is no special legal protection for them, and if the community dispenses with their services, they must surrender their advantages. The chaukidar alone is an exception. Under the Chief Commissioner's Circular, 16 of 1862, para. 13, where a village chaukidar was found to be remunerated by rent-free land or land held at a low rent, the Settlement Officer was directed to record the holding and the terms on which it was held as an incident in the tenure of the village, but he was not to set aside any land for him in addition, and former orders were modified accordingly. This land cannot be resumed at the will of the landlord, unless and until the chaukidar is dismissed by order of the Deputy Commissioner, who alone has power to do so. In such case, as the tenure is a service one, I apprehend that the chaukidar, if dispossessed at once, would be entitled to compensation for the crop in the ground, or he might hold until the rabi harvest; but in that case he would have to pay rent to the landlord for the time that he was not chaukidar. In respect of any land not recorded in the settlement papers, the chaukidar is on the footing of an ordinary tenant; but if the land is held as wages, and the landlord should eject him, the rules and the landlord's kabuliat provide that the Deputy Commissioner may collect the cess at the rate of six per cent. on the revenue and pay the chaukidar in cash.

CHAPTER II.

MUTATIONS.

THE mutation of a name in the malguzari register, if it means anything, implies that the Collector is henceforward to collect the revenue from the person whose name is substituted for that of the person formerly liable. By the people it is looked upon as a regular and legal transfer of the property, and even in a legal point of view it gives the person whose name is entered all the advantages of possession as it is supposed to be the record of an existing fact. The law, which was enacted in Section 21, Regulation VIII of 1800, and re-enacted in Regulation XLII of 1803, and is stated in paras. 187 and 192 of the Directions to Collectors, which is law in Oudh, affirms that mutation must follow transfer, and para. 200 does not seem to leave the Collector any discretion in the matter. I apprehend that if a mutation had been made in the malguzari register, and the old malguzar had lost possession of the land, should the Collector still demand the revenue from the old malguzar, the Civil Court would protect him from it on application. This law was originally made for Bengal, where a most rigid law of sale obtains in default of payment of the revenue, and to that state of affairs it is suited; but it is not suited to such a revenue system as is in force in the province of Oudh.

The following case not very long ago occurred in my own experience. A coparcenary community had mortgaged a chak of their village, on which chak a separate assessment was made by the Settlement Officer, though it was under one engagement with the village for the revenue. The zemindars, feeling they could not redeem the chak, and indeed not intending to do so, neglected it, and it fell out of cultivation. They did not pay the mortgagee, who sued on his bond, got a decree, and sold the chak in execution, and the auction-purchaser got a mutation of the chak made in his own name in the malguzari register. On going into the affairs of his purchase, however, the auction-purchaser found the rental of the chak would not pay the revenue assessed upon it, and he applied for a revision of jama, which was refused, as the assessment was a perfectly fair one at the time it was made. It appeared to me however, that the Government would have lost its revenue had the auction-purchaser proved a man of straw. I was told in this case by superior authority, that the Deputy Commissioner did wrong in making this mutation, that in the malguzari register mutation should be made of lambardars only, and that the mutation should only have been made in the village khewat which would have left the joint responsibility in tact. This is, no doubt, what was intended in the Directions, but it is very far from disposing of the difficulties of the case in the North-Western Provinces, as far as I can see, and still less in Oudh. The mutation in the khewat transfers the jama as well as the land, and is as binding individually among the parties entered in it as the malguzari register is between the whole community and the Government; and as the auction-purchaser was not, and, as a rule, is not a man of straw, he had no redress against the fraud of the zemindars: he was equally liable for the jama within the community as without it, though the

Government was protected from loss had he been a man of straw. But how if the zemindar had been a talukdar, the owner of a hundred villages, and no khewat in which to make mutation? It cannot be contended that he is not free to sell one, and under the compulsory law of mutation the Deputy Commissioner must make the mutation and free the talukdar from his liability. But supposing this village was the dídári of a former zemindar and rent-free, and the purchaser was a man of straw, who, his work being done, disappeared; the talukdar would have got rid of his obligation to pay the revenue on it, and the Deputy Commissioner would come down on the under-proprietor and practically confiscate half his property. I put an extreme case to make it more clear, but this objection applies to every bit of sír or other under-proprietary right held at a rent less than the Government revenue assessed upon it.

But the fact is that mutations of the liability for the revenue of parts of villages are made not unfrequently in the malguzari register, and, as a general rule, it is for the interest of Government that they should be made. A pattidar mortgages his patti to a stranger, who is a man of substance, and gives him posssession. The community, though not yet driven to part with their land, are not flourishing, and the stranger will only take the patti on condition of a mutation. He is not going to make himself jointly and severally liable for the revenue on all the other shares. I say in such a case, and every revenue officer knows how common it is, the interests of all parties are best consulted by making the mutation. All these difficulties are disposed of by giving practical application to the great principle stated in the introduction " that the owner of an estate pay-
" ing revenue to Government cannot relieve himself of the

"obligation to pay the revenue on any part of it without "the consent of Government, unless by parting with the "whole property." To give practical application to this, a mutation in the malguzari register must not be "the declaration of an existing fact," but a high act of discretion on the part of the Deputy Commissioner subject to appeal to the judgment of his revenue superiors.

CHAPTER III.

SURFACE, CLIMATE, AND SOILS.

THE surface of Oudh is level, the whole province being in the alluvial plain of the Ganges and the Gogra with their tributaries. Here and there it gently undulates but very slightly, and the chief differences of surface are between the low land bordering the large rivers, called *tarai, ganjar, kádir, mánjha,* and *kach* in different parts of the province, and the land above the high bank of the rivers called *bangar,* and in some place *bhur*. The province, as a whole, is well cultivated and beautifully wooded. Mango groves predominate, but in some parts, especially Pratabgarh, the mhowa is very common, and pakar, gular, pipal, jáman, and tamarind are found everywhere, besides many other trees in lesser numbers. Bamboos are rather scarce: they are, I believe, capricious about the soil they grow in, but still there are quite enough scattered over the province to show that, with a little pains, much more might be made of this most useful and beautiful tree. There is not a twentieth part of what there might be of land under that useful and profitable tree the babul. Water is abundant everywhere, and, as a rule, near the surface. In many parts the kacha well stands for years, and in those parts the cultivation is generally of a high class.

Between the lines of the principal rivers, that is, between the Gogra and the Gumti, the Gumti and the Sai, and the Sai and the Ganges, there are lines of jhils which are largely used for irrigation. The water of these jhils is not considered so good for irrigation purposes as that from wells; but it has not to be raised so far, and the increased quantity makes it sought for, the rather that in the jhil region the wells will not stand unless built of something or other, and where they are used, they are usually constructed of rough segmental burnt bricks without any mortar. Regular masonry wells for purposes of irrigation, though far from being unknown, are not common, but they are increasing. Nevertheless, Oudh is one of the best watered provinces of India, and the south-eastern half of the province has a more than ordinary proportion of irrigated land.

The climate of Oudh is healthy, and one of the best in the plains of India. It has a hot season, a rainy season, and a cold season. The hot season commences in the south of Oudh towards the end of March, and lasts until the rains begin generally from the 20th to the 30th June. The early half of this is not unpleasant, but the month before the rains is oppressively hot. The rains in Oudh are more constant, showery, and seldom come down in such continued torrents as elsewhere, and the breaks are pleasanter there being more wind than across the Ganges. The close of the rains is the most unhealthy period of the year. In some parts of the province, notably in the terai lands, there is much fever at this season. The cold weather, from the middle of October to March, is almost a perfect climate. Bright sunshine, clear crisp air, and a cold sufficient to stimulate without causing any suffering make camp life at this season delightful. It never feels too cold as in the Panjab, nor is there the rain that often falls in that province at this season. The cold weather rain in Oudh seldom lasts more than three days, and the weather is deliciously cold after it. The people of the country, when adequately fed, show a fine physique; but the population is so great that there is a large proportion of underfed among them.

The soils at the settlement were virtually divided by official instructions into *matiar, domat,* and *bhur.* Matiar was supposed to be a clayey soil, bhur a sandy soil, and domat a mixture of the two in varying proportions. Real matiar, such as is found in the sugar lands of Azimgarh and Ghazipur, is not common in Oudh, and the name is often given to a stiff low-lying soil, which, in eastern Oudh, is called *bijar.* This is rice soil, though sometimes a second crop, generally gram, is sown in it. Bhur is a name applied to all sandy soils, from those little better than sandhills, in which only *mot* will grow, to soils hardly to be distinguished from domat, and when irrigated bearing very fine crops. The soil, however, most distinctively bhur, yields as a rule *bájra* and barley, and is generally dependent for its moisture on the rains and dews of heaven alone. This kind of soil requires frequent rest. It is half the time fallow, and the breadth of it cultivated in a given year depends so much on circumstances that very careful consideration of them is necessary to the assessing officer. In my experience it is generally in this class of soil that assessments break down in bangar villages.

The best land in Oudh goes by the name of domat, but of this soil there are great varieties. In south-eastern Oudh as a rule it is irrigated, but not so in the north. The rains, however, in the north are perhaps steadier, the lands being nearer to the hills, nevertheless the produce is certainly lighter to the acre. This soil is more extensively distributed than any other, and it is easily cultivated and may be relied on to produce a fair average succession of crops. It is unquestionably the easiest for the assessing officer to deal with, and with ordinary care he should seldom make a mistake with respect to it.

But there are other soils which hardly come under these denominations. The first of these is *Goind* or *Gauhan*. This is the irrigated and manured land generally about the village site or those of its hamlets. It is, however, to be remembered that the site of a village may be on its own border, and in such case the adjoining lands, though situated in another village, may be really goind on account of the neighbourhood of a village site. This land is, of course, the best of all and pays the highest rate of rent, and where there are káchis and moraos among the village cultivators, is usually occupied by them for the simple reason that they will give much more for it. They raise principally tobacco, poppy, vegetables, and potatoes, crops grown on lands paying high rents where the rent system is money, and special money rents for the season in which such crops are raised where the rent system is corn. This will be more fully explained when we come to treat of rents.

In the terai lands, the soil is subject to constant change from the action of rivers. I do not mean only to change from increment or decrement, but to changes in the quality of the soil itself induced by fluvial action. This soil is, as a rule, cold and wet, and it varies very greatly in depth. Sometimes it is only a few inches deep with a bed of sand below, and the crop grown upon it, which looks a beautiful one when it is five or six inches high, having thrust its roots through the thin soil becomes stunted and very light in its later stage of development. Sometimes the deposit is several feet thick, and the rabi crops produced are very fine indeed; but the uncertainty of the kharif crop and the ever present possibility of a flood deposit of sand make a flourishing rabi harvest an unsafe guide in such lands. The mode in which floods act upon them is generally as follows:—The Oudh rivers; which come from the hills, the Ganges, Gambira or Ramganga, Chauka, Ghogra, and Rapti, bring down in flood a silt composed of two elements, sand which when deposited is destructive, *pan* which when deposited is fertilizing. So long as the water is rushing on at a certain velocity both are held in suspension; but as soon as water surcharged with this silt overflows the banks and the flow becomes checked, it begins to deposit. Now the sand is heavier than the pan and lodges first, and it becomes deposited in a current which is strong enough to carry away the pan. Hence, if the overflowed bank rises gently inwards, the sand will be deposited nearest to the bed of the river, and the pan on the higher land beyond; but if, as often is the case, the immediate bank is higher and there is a hollow beyond, the flow of the water will at once choose the lower level where the sand will be deposited, and the pan will be lodged on the higher intermediate ground. This accounts for the frequent sandy beds we find inland on the kádirs of large rivers which are locally termed *sotas*, and which are the first filled with water in a flood. It is, however, to be remembered that any one of these sotas may become the main river in one of its flood freaks, and though a Settlement Officer is not expected to anticipate changes of such magnitude, which must be dealt with specially at the time of occurrence, he would not fail to draw attention to the contingency to account for the possible failure of his assessment from such a cause in the future.

The classification of soils is an exceedingly difficult matter, and requires the combined knowledge of the chemist and the local practical agriculturist. The variety is very great, and the changes very sudden. Indeed this is acknowledged in para. 64 of the Directions to Settlement Officers. Though these officers are instructed to assess "mainly on the products of the cultivated land" (para. 56), they are yet told, in para. 50, that the "ascertainment of "the net produce of an estate is a fallacious basis on which "alone to found any certain determination of the demand. "It is itself difficult to accomplish, and the attempt to effect "it is likely to produce many serious evils." In fact the North-Western assessments have been made on rent rates applied to classified soils, and those of Oudh also for the most part; but those assessments which have been founded on hárs have been more successful than those founded on soils as far as my experience goes. *Hárs* form a classification dependent on the distance of the lands from the inhabited village, and are usually divided into inlying, outlying, and intermediate. As a rule, this gives a practical distinction; and with occasional exceptions, the rents will be found to vary as the distance of the cultivated land from the village.

CHAPTER IV.
CROPS.

THERE are three regular crops in Oudh besides some special ones. They are called *Kharif, Hewant,* and *Rabi.* The special crops are chiefly sugar, which is planted in April and cut in February; indigo, which is in the ground two years; and cotton. Of these sugar is a staple of some importance, the growth of the other two is trifling and I believe diminishing. The ordinary kharif crops are—

Dhán ushan	...	Broadcast rice.
Makai	...	Maize.
Kodu	...	(*Paspalum frumentaceum.*)
Kákun.		
Makra.		
Sáwan	...	(*Panicum frumentaceum.*)

These crops are sown with the first rains, and reaped in August and September. The ordinary hewant crops are—

Dhán Jarhan	...	Transplanted rice.
Jauár	...	(*Holcus Sorghum.*)
Bájra		(*Holcus spicatus.*)
Urd or *másh*	...	(*Phaseolus radiatus.*)
Mung	...	(*Phaseolus mungo.*)
Mot.		
Til	...	(*Sesamum orientale.*)
Patua.		

These crops are sown in August, generally in a break of the rains, and are reaped either in November or December. Jarhan rice is sown broadcast with the first fall of rain, and is transplanted in August.

The ordinary rabi crops are—

Alu	Potatoes (*Solamium Tuberosum*).
Ghíun ...	Wheat.
Gajai	Wheat and barley.
Jau ...	Barley.
Birra or *bijri* ...	Barley and peas or gram.
Arhar ...	(*Cytisus cajan*.)
Channa ...	Gram (*Cicer arietinum*).
Matar ...	Peas.
Kasári ...	Chickling vetch (*Lathyrus Sativus*).
Massur ...	Lentils (*Cicer Lens*).
Alsi ...	Linseed.
Sarson ...	Mustard.
Láhi ...	Rapeseed (*Brassica Napus*).
Kusam ...	Safflower (*Carthamus tinctorius*).
Rámdána.	

These crops are sown in October, and reaped, according to the locality, from the end of February to the beginning of May. Arhar is an exception: it is sown at the beginning of rains, and cut in April.

Though the above are the principal crops, they are far from being the whole. Thus, vegetables are grown all the year round in great variety; tobacco and poppy in the cold weather; melons, another kind of sáwan, and Jeth rice in the hot weather; besides a number of aromatic seeds, such as dhania (coriander), jira (cumin), sounf (anise), &c.; as also roots, such as haldi (turmeric), and others which it is not necessary to mention, as they do not influence the assessment of the land revenue. They are cut when the hot weather comes on.

The crops are sown ekfasli, dofasli, or utér. *Ekfasli* is where only one crop is sown in the land during the year. *Dofasli* is where two crops are sown in the same land in succession to each other. *Utér* is when two crops are sown together and reaped at different times. Thus arhar, which is a long time in the ground, is almost invariably sown utér, as is also often cotton. Kodu is sown utér generally with arhar. So also mustard with wheat, safflower and wheat, linseed and gram, &c. Of course the crops that are grown and cut together, such as *gujai, birra,* and gram and *kasári,* do not come within this category.

Although a crop grown ekfasli will produce far more than the same crop grown dofasli, yet as a rule the yearly yield of dofasli land is the greater. But all these things, when the Settlement Officer has to deal with corn rents, require careful and anxious study. It is manifest that so long as he neglects them he cannot rightly estimate the produce of his lands, nor can he duly and satisfactorily compare produce with area, for though many of the lands produce two crops in the same year as has been shown, the putwáris never show the area twice, and consequently the second or rabi crop is made to appear to grow on a smaller area than in reality, and a higher rate of rent would be deduced from the actual rents of it.

CHAPTER V.

RENT.

THERE is a considerable variety in the way of calculating and expressing rent in the province of Oudh, but rent may be broadly divided into money rents, corn rents, and mixed rents.

1. Fixed rent.
2. Ordinary money rent.
3. Katti.
4. Zabti.
5. Nijkari.

} *Money rents (Jamai).*

6. Batai.
7. Kankut.

} *Corn rents (Ghallai).*

8. Darkatti.
9. Thahrai.
10. Nakshi.

} *Mixed rents (Jamai).*

SECTION I.—MONEY RENTS.

Fixed rent.—Fixed rent may be of three kinds; 1st, rent fixed by decree of court for ever; 2nd, rent fixed by decree of court for the term of the settlement; 3rd, rent fixed by decree of court for five years. The first kind of rent is applicable to under-proprietary rights alone. The second is applicable to under-proprietary rights, and also to some of the rights of occupancy created under the Chief Commissioner's Revenue Circular No. 16 of 1874, with the difference in the last mentioned case that the rent is fixed by the act of Government in virtue of its proprietary right and not by decree of court. The third kind is applicable to other rights of occupancy. There is one other temporarily fixed rent, namely, 'parmsána,' which is the rent reserved in the 'biswi' tenure, under which heading it will be found described. It of course ceases, or rather merges, in the full rent on the redemption of the 'biswi' mortgage by the zemindar mortgagor. All fixed rents are more or less favored rents (riayatti), they are not the full rent of the land, and it is a principle of assessment that they are liable to enhancement for the purpose of fixing the Government demand.

Ordinary money rent.—Ordinary money rent is money rent which is a matter of bargain between landlord and tenant. It is influenced partly by custom, partly by competition, partly by the pressure of population on the land, and partly by the will and influence of the parties to the transaction. It may be held to represent the landlord's share of the produce adjusted for an average of years and seasons by those who know most about it. Where these rents prevail they seldom vary on old, good, inlying lands.*

They are more fluctuating on new outlying lands. More subject to climatic influences. Nevertheless, they are the surest and most reliable data from which to value lands for the purposes of assessment, and the Settlement Officer is fortunate who finds them to work upon. These rents, when once settled, even in outlying lands, change with difficulty, and usually last for some years.

Katti is an ordinary true money rent. The tenant can raise whatever crop he likes as in the two former cases without reference to his rent, but it is essentially a tentative rent, and appears to me to be an endeavour by the landlord to turn corn into money rent. It is a feature

---

* It is curious that this is also true at home. I was told by one of the leading farmers in Banffshire that the rent of such lands in that country and Aberdeen had not varied for 70 years; and by one of the leading farmers of Morayshire, where good farming began earlier, they had not there varied for 100 years. Yet in no part of Great Britain has farming improved more than in these counties. The improvement has all been in the outlying and waste lands.

of it that either party, though bound by it for the year agreed upon, may revert to corn rent at its close. It is low in proportion to corn rent as would be expected, but though tenants sometimes stick to it for several good years, a bad one frightens them, and they are apt to revert to corn rent. This rent, so far as I know, is peculiar to the parganahs liable to the fluvial action of the Chauka and Ghagra rivers in Kheri. Rent is not, I believe, known by that name on similar lands in Sitapur.

Zabti.—This word is not in use in this province so far as I know. The rents which I describe under this name are called 'jamai;' but that word means any cash rent and is not sufficiently distinctive, so I have adopted this word, which I find in the Directions to Settlement Officers (App. XIII-C) to signify a peculiar class of rent. *Zabti* is a special rent paid on a special crop, but only paid when that crop is grown. The special crops are usually sugarcane, tobacco, potatoes, poppy, turmeric, and vegetables. There is a fixed rate for each in the village which does not vary, but the rate for none of them is the same, and it is only paid when that particular crop is cultivated.

Nijkari.—In the Directions this word is used to mean the corn rent paid by the cultivating proprietor when he does not grow a *zabti* crop. In the Kheri District however the word is used to signify the money rent paid by a tenant under the same circumstances. If he pays a corn rent it is called batai. Nijkari means the alternative rent paid with the zabti, and is not used except on lands where the latter rent is paid in some years. There is no doubt a rotation of zabti, and nijkari or batai, but I cannot say what it is, nor do I believe it is even ordinarily adhered to, as the growth of zabti crops depends largely on the caste of the cultivators, the capital they have at command, and the price of the article to be raised. It is evident that to draw *data* for assessment from such rents as these requires great care and the average of a considerable number of years. To assess on rent rates formed from them on the area of a single year would most probably end in a break down, unless it was pitched so low as to do manifest injustice to Government.

Section II.—CORN RENTS.

Batai.—Batai is the actual division of the garnered crop between landlord and tenant. It is a common form of rent in the province, and has customs connected with it of a complicated character and varying in different estates. I here only pretend to give some of them. The rate of division is generally expressed as a half, a third, or a fourth to the landlord, but these rates are far from indicating the real shares. There are numerous wages, expenses, and dues deducted from balances which are left at certain stages of the process, and then added to the shares of either landlord or tenant as the case may be, and some are given to outsiders. The following is a list of these as far as I know:

No.	Name of deduction.	Amount of deduction.	To whom given.	What the deduction is.
1	Bísar	One-fortieth	Chaukidar.	The allowance to the chaukidar or goreit for watching the crops. It is sometimes left standing in the field for the man to cut himself; sometimes, however, it is given at the threshing-floor, and then it is a seer in the maund.

No.	Name of deduction.	Amount of deduction.	To whom given.	What the deduction is.
2	Loni	About one-thirteenth of what is left when the bisar is not cut to about one-seventeenth when it is.	The reapers.	Each reaper places the ears he has cut in a heap and the assámi counts them by handfuls, giving each seventeenth handful to the reaper. Sometimes it is done by estimate. If the assámi and his family reaped, they get their share. The higher rate is given in Kheri, the lower in Sitapur.
3	Lahna or Parja or Dabi.	Varies, it is so much per plough.	Blacksmith, Carpenter, Dhobi, Chamar, Nau.	These dues are paid in unthreshed ears of grain, and do not appear in the account of the batai. These three are deducted from the divisible produce before the grain is threshed out. After that process comes
4	Charwa	Varies from 2 to 4 seers per maund on the grain threshed out.	Tenant or herd if he employs one.	The herd's wages. The calculation on the grain threshed out is not uniform as will appear in the examples. It is sometimes calculated on the united shares of the landlord and tenant after all the deductions have been made, and sometimes on them at an earlier stage.
5	Kúr	Varies from 5½ to 7½ seers per maund on the balance after deducting the charwa.	Tenant...	The ploughman's wages. The rest of the remark on charwa applies to kúr also. This allowance is not always given. In Parganah Goudlamau no case of it was found.
6	Shaina	Usually 1 seer per maund on the united shares.	Landlord	The wages of the cropwatcher, the man placed by the landlord to prevent its removal until the rent is paid. In Parganah Gondlamau the following custom is said to prevail. Where the field is large, not less than an acre or so, the tenant cuts a biswa, the whole grain of which he keeps. In lieu of this he pays 5 kacha seers after the batai to the shaina. Then it does not appear in the threshing-floor account.

No.	Name of deduction.	Amount of deduction.	To whom given.	What the deduction is.
7	Patwári	Ditto	Landlord	The wages of the village accountant. Sometimes the patwári collects this himself, but generally it is credited.
8	Tolai	A half seer per maund on the united shares.	Ditto	This is supposed to be the wages of the man who weighs out the corn, but sometimes it becomes a mere perquisite, and there is another charge for weighing as in Specimens Nos. 3 and 4. In Specimens Nos. 1 and 2 this is 1 seer per maund.
9	Dharrah	Ditto	Ditto	This is for the hire of scales and weights.
10	Pai	Half the tolai	Ditto	A pure perquisite.
11	Tappa	Same as tolai	Ditto	A charge for scaling the crop when threshed out and before weighing.
12	Khorák amla.	Same as pai	Landlord's agent.	A perquisite of the landlord's agent.
13	Anjuri	Varies, about 3 seers in 5 maunds.	Sometimes landlord, sometimes tenant.	Means as much grain as can be held in the two hands. It is sometimes thrown more than once on the landlord's heap, but in Gondlamau the following account of it is given: Before the weighing begins, the cultivator takes out of the whole heap a basketful of grain which he distributes on the threshing-floor in several small heaps, usually seven, eight, or nine. One of these is for himself, and one for his special god; these two are as large as all the rest put together. He puts one for the particular mahaut, fakir, or bhát who receives fees from the village, one for the máli, one for the pási, and one for the dihiwál, who lights the fire at the holi.

No.	Name of deduction.	Amount of deduction.	To whom given.	What the deduction is.
14	Kathri	Varies	Half to landlord and half to tenant.	The remainder of what is separated from the main heap. In the examples, Nos. 3 and 5, given, it is the remainder after the deductions have taken place, but in Gondlamau it is described as follows:— When the grain is about to be threshed, the tenant selects some of the finest ears for seed. These are kept in ear till seed time, and are called *bisára*. But there is always some grain left in the threshed ears and chaff which is called *bhúlan*. Of course it is the tenant's business to make this as much as possible, and his efforts are to a certain extent winked at. Besides this the tenant takes a certain portion of the threshed out grain, and ostentatiously hides it under some chaff—this is called *nakol*. This portion, the bhúlan and the bisára, form the kathri. The patwári then makes an estimate of this, always favorable to the tenant, and deducts the charwa therefrom, for the charwa is included in the kathri where this custom prevails, and half of the remainder is assigned to the landlord. The tenant then pays this assignment from his own heap of grain to the landlord and takes all the kathri.
15	Tari	A quarter to a half seer per maund.	Tenant	Is connected with the word 'tarai,' and means what is below underneath. It is the grain that is left on the floor at the weighing and swept up. Only reported to me from Parganah Gondlamau.

These deductions are probably far from exhaustive, though they are all that I have been able to hear of. They are not all in use in the same village, as the following specimen batais will show:—

SPECIMEN No. 1.

Agarbazurg Estate. Parganah Bhur. District Kheri.
Half and half batai.

	Mds.	Seers.
Total outturn	20	0
Deduct Loni	1	20
Remainder ...	18	20
Charwa at 2 seers per maund on last remainder	0	37
Remainder ...	17	23
Kúr at 6½ seers on last remainder ...	2	28½
	14	34½

Expenses at 4 seers per maund, *viz.* :—

	Seers.		
Shaina at 1 seer per maund on last remainder	14¾		
Patwári ditto ditto ...	14¼		
Tolai ditto ditto ...	14¾		
Village expenses ...	15¼		
		1	19½

United shares ...	13	15

Cultivator.			*Landlord.*		
	Mds.	Seers.		Mds.	Seers
Share ...	6	27½	Share ...	6	27½
Loni ...	1	20	Expenses ...	1	19½
Charwa ...	0	37			
Kur ...	2	28½	Real share ...	8	7
Real share ...	11	33			

	Mds.	Seers.
Landlord ...	8	7
Tenant ...	11	33
Total ...	20	0

SPECIMEN No. 2.

Agarbazurg, Estate. Parganah Bhur, District Kheri.
One-third to the landlord with 4 seers charwa.

	Mds.	Seers.
Total outturn	20	0
Loni	1	20
Remainder	18	20
Charwa 4 seers on last remainder	1	34
Remainder	16	26
Kúr at 6½ seers on last remainder	2	24
	14	2

Expenses at 4 seers on last remainder:

	Seers.		
Shaina at 1 seer ditto	14		
Patwári ditto	14		
Tolai ditto	14		
Village expenses	14		
	—	1	16
United shares		12	26

Tenant.				Landlord.			
	Mds.	Srs.	Ch.		Mds.	Srs.	Ch.
Share	8	17	4	Share	4	8	12
Loni	1	20	0	Expenses	1	16	0
Charwa	1	34	0				
Kúr	2	24	0	Real share	5	24	12
Real share	14	15	4				

	Mds.	Srs.	Ch.
Landlord	5	24	12
Tenant	14	15	4
Total	20	0	0

SPECIMEN No. 3.

Agarbazurg Estate.   Pargana Bhur.   District Kheri.
One-third to the landlord with 4 seers charwa.

		Mds.	Seers.
Total outturn	... ...	20	0
Deduct Loni	... ...	1	20
		18	20

Weigh out by guess :—

		Mds.	Srs.		
Landlord's share	...	4	0		
Tenant's ditto	...	8	0		
United shares		12	0		
Kúr at 7½ on united share	...	2	10		
Charwa at 4 ditto	...	1	8		
				3	18

Expense as detailed

		Seers.		
Patwári at 1 seer on united shares		12		
Shainah at 1 seer ditto	...	12		
Village expenses at 1 seer ditto	...	12		
Darrah at ½ seer ditto	...	6		
Tolai at ½ seer ditto	...	6		
Tappah at ½ seer ditto	...	6		
Total expenses	...		1	14
Weighman	... ...		0	6
Actually paid	...		16	38
Remainder	...		1	22

This remainder is called the kathri, and is divided, two-thirds to the tenant and one-third to the landlord. The final shares are :

Landlord.			*Tenant.*			*Actual Division.*		
	Mds.	Srs.		Mds.	Srs.		Mds.	Srs.
Share ...	4	0	Share ...	8	0	Landlord ...	5	34⅔
Expenses	1	14	Kúr ...	2	10	Tenant ..	13	39⅓
Kathri ...	0	20⅔	Loni ...	1	20	Weighman ...	0	6
			Charwa	1	8			
Total ...	5	34⅔	Kathri ...	0	41⅓	Grand Total	20	0½
			Total ...	13	39⅓			

SPECIMEN No. 4.

Agarbazury Estate. Parganah Bhur. District Kheri.
One-half to landlord with 2 seers charwa.

		Mds.	Seers.
Total outturn	...	20	0
Loni	...	1	20
Remainder	...	18	20

	Mds.	Srs.	Chks.
United shares	13	28	0

Tenant.

	Mds.	Srs.	Chks.			
Share ...	6	34	0			
Kúr 7½ seers on the united shares	2	18	8			
Charwa 2 seers ditto	0	27	0			
				9	39	8

Landlord.

	Mds.	Srs.	Chks.			
Share ...	6	34	0			
Shaina 1 seer on the united shares	0	13	5⅓			
Patwári ditto ...	0	13	5⅓			
Village expenses ditto	0	13	5⅓			
Tolai ½ seer ditto	0	6	10			
Durrah ditto ditto	0	6	10			
Tappah ditto ditto	0	6	10			
				8	13	14
Weighman	...	0	6	10		
				18	20	

Landlord.				Tenant.				Actual division.			
	Md.	Sr.	Ch.		Md.	Sr.	Ch.		Md.	Sr.	Ch.
Share ...	6	34	0	Share	6	34	0	Landlord	8	13	14
Expenses.	1	19	14	Loni ...	1	20	0	Tenant	11	19	8
				Kúr ...	2	18	8	Weighman	0	6	10
Total ...	8	13	14	Charwa	0	27	0	Grand Total	20	0	0
				Total ...	11	19	8				

In this batai the weighman has hit it off so exactly that I should have suspected its being a genuine one but that he has taken some slight liberty in the calculation of the charges on the united shares.

CHAP. V.] CORN RENTS. 71

SPECIMEN No. 5.

Raipur Estate Parganah Haiderabad. District Kheri.
One-half to the landlord with 2 seers charwa.

		Mds.	Srs.
Total produce	...	21	0

Measure out—

		Mds.	Seers.		
Landlord's share	... ...	9	0		
Tenant's share ...	... ...	9	0		
				18	0
Remainder	...			3	0

Deduct—

		Srs.		
Patwári 1 seer per maund on the united shares	... ...	11		
Village expenses ditto	... ...	18		
Tolai ½ ditto ∴	... ...	9		
Khorák Amla ¼ ditto	... ...	4½		
Pai ¼ ditto	... ...	4½		
Charwa	... ...	36	2	10
Remainder	...		0	30

This remainder is called the kathri, and is divided equally between the landlord and the tenant. Their final shares stand thus:—

Landlord.			Tenant.		
	Mds.	Seers.		Mds.	Seers.
Share ...	9	0	Share ...	9	0
Expenses ...	1	14	Charwa ...	0	36
Half kathri ...	0	15	Half kathri ...	0	11
Total ...	10	29	Total ...	10	11

		Mds.	Seers.
Total of landlord	... ...	10	29
Ditto tenant	... ...	10	11
Grand Total	...	21	0

SPECIMEN No. 6.

Mauzah Gondlamau. Parganah Gondlamau. District Sitapur.
Debi Gureria's batai.

This was an actual batai made before the officer who reported it. It is a one-half batai with village expenses, calculated at 2¼ seers, and bisar at 1 seer per maund on the united shares as first weighed, charwa at 2 seers on the total united shares, and hak zemindari at 5 seers on the tenant's share of the total united shares, plus his calculated share of the kathri. The batai was as follows:—

There was no bisára, and the bhúlan was estimated at 10 seers. The tenant then set aside the nakd estimated at 20 seers, and the anjuri at 4 seers.

	Mds.	Seers.
Then was weighed landlord's share	2	30
Ditto tenant	2	30
United shares as first weighed	5	20
On this was calculated and weighed out—		
Village expenses at 2¼ seers	0	12½
Bisar ditto 1 seer	0	5½
	0	18

These were taken by those entitled to them. The remainder was then weighed.

	Mds.	Seers.
Landlord's share	0	7
Tenant's share	0	7
Second weighment of united shares	0	14
Total united shares	5	34

There remained the tari, which was estimated at 3 seers. There was the kathri, which amounted to

	Mds.	Seers.
Bhulan	0	10
Nakd	0	20
Kathri	0	30

[CHAP. V.] CORN RENTS. 73

The Charwa, which in this batai comes out of the kathri, was then calculated on the total united shares. It comes to a little less than 12 seers, but was fixed at that. The account then stood for the kathri

	Mds.	Seers.
Charwa	0	12
Landlord's share	0	9
Tenant's share	0	9
Total kathri	0	30

Nine seers were then taken from the tenant's heap by weighment and put on the landlord's. The tenant took the whole kathri.

The tenant's share then stood by the account—

	Mds.	Seers.
First weighment	2	30
Second ditto	0	7
Half kathri by account	0	9
Total	3	6

On this the hak zemindari was calculated. The odd six seers were not assessed, and 15 seers was fixed as the amount. The 15 seers were placed from the tenant's heap on to the landlord's. The final account then stood—

	Mds.	Seers.
Landlord's total weighed out share	2	37
First deduction from tenant kathri	0	9
Second ditto ditto hak zemindari	0	15
	3	21

	Mds.	Seers.		Mds.	Seers.
Tenant's weighed out share	2	37			
Less deducted for landlord	0	24			
			2	13	
Tari			0	3	
Kathri			0	30	
				3	6
Village expenses				0	12½
Bisar				0	5½
Anjur				0	4
Grand Total				7	9

10

SPECIMEN No. 7.

Mauzah Pati Newáda. Parganah Gondlamau. District Sitapur.

Dhanrinjna chamar's batai made in a similar way to the last with village expenses 2 seers per maund.

	Mds.	Seers.
Landlord got	2	$13\frac{1}{2}$
Tenant got	2	3
Village expenses and bisar	0	$10\frac{1}{2}$
Anjuri	0	$2\frac{1}{2}$
Total	4	$29\frac{1}{2}$

The tari in this case was $1\frac{1}{2}$ seers. The kathri was appraised at 10 seers nakd and 5 seers bhulan.

SPECIMEN No. 8.

Mauzah Gondlamau Kháss. Parganah Gondlamau. District Sitapur.

Lálta Singh's batai.

No hak zemindari was taken, the tenant got 2 seers charwa, and the village expenses were $2\frac{1}{4}$ seers, bisar as usual.

	Mds.	Seers.
Landlord got	6	35
Tenant got	7	30
Village expenses and bisar	0	$35\frac{3}{4}$
Anjuri	0	6
Total	15	$26\frac{3}{4}$

The tari in this was 10 seers. The kathri was appraised at 1 maund nakd, 1 maund and 10 seers bhulan, and 15 seers bisára. Total kathri 2 maunds 25 seers.

SPECIMEN No. 9.

Purwa Harhiharpur.   Mauzah Dharauli.   Parganah Gondlamau. District Sitapur.

Lálla Dhobi's batai. One share to the landlord and two to the tenant. No hak zemindari or charwa; village expenses 2¼ seers per maund on the united shares. Bisar is as usual.

	Mds.	Seers.
Landlord's share	1	17
Tenant's share	3	5¼
Village expenses and bisar	0	12
Anjuri	0	3
	4	37¾

The tari was 1½ seers. In the kathri no nakd or bisára was allowed: the bhulan was estimated at 10 seers, and being so small nothing was taken from his heap on account of the landlord's kathri.

SPECIMEN No. 10.

Mauzah Buhra Khera   Parganah Misrikh.   District Sitapur.

Debi Brahmin's batai. Kúr 7½ seers per maund, and charwa 2 seers on the united shares. The village expenses were on the united shares plus the kúr.

	Mds.	Seers.
Landlord got	17	17½
Tenant got	25	25
Village expenses	3	5
Anjuri	0	10
	46	17½

The kathri was 8 maunds, and the assámi got 1 maund 35 seers remitted in the appraisement of it. The landlord took half the village expenses in addition to what is put down to him, so that his real share was 19 maunds.

In parts of Kheri and Sitapur, there is a custom known as 'dolakh,' which was a device to cheat the Government under the native system of annual assessments, and considerably affected batai rents. It was discovered in some Government villages in which the patwáris had used it to cheat the tahsildár, and the system was fully disclosed in a trial of one of the Sarbarakárs of the encumbered estates for embezzlement.

Dolakh means two weighments, and appears to be derived from *do*, two, and *lakhna*, to weigh or ascertain. In the case disclosed, it was worked as follows:—An addition of 1½ seers was added to the bottom of the dharrah or weight of 15 seers. The grain was weighed first with the false weight and this alone was shown to the Government officer, but when his back was turned, the addition was removed from the dharrah, and the grain was weighed with the true weight. The difference was then divided between the landlord and the tenant as shown in Specimen No. 5, but the following items were omitted from the account in question, and were embezzled by the Sarbarakar.

| Khorák Shaina. | Charwa. |
| Pai. | Kathri. |

The khorák shaina was a charge of 5 seers per tenant, which was deducted from each tenant's share. In consequence of this, the shares were shown thus:—

	Mds.	Seers.
Landlord	10	5
Tenant	9	0
Weighed false by dolakh	19	5

while under the true weight the division would have been—

	Mds.	Seers.
Landlord	11	30
Tenant	9	10
Total	21	0

It was the greed of the Sarbarakar which caused his detection. He appropriated the whole difference 1 maund 35 seers. Had he given the tenants their 10 seers of the dolakh, he would probably have escaped detection.

In some villages subject to fluvial action, the waters overspread the land and generate weeds and strong coarse grasses in baneful luxuriance. There the cultivation is constantly changing, and the rate of batai changes with it after the fashion of nakshi rents to be hereafter described.

In one such village these causes necessitate a change of cultivation on the average every fourth year. New land is then broken and the rate becomes,

First year, one-twelfth.
Second year, one-sixth.
Third year, one-third.

After this when it is abandoned, a new area is taken up in lieu thereof at one-twelfth. In another village there were three rates—one-half, two-fifths, and one-third. A tenant in this village, holding at one-half batai and changing his land, paid one-third for the first year, and one-half thenceforward until he changed again. One holding at two-fifths, changing his land, paid one-third the first year, and two-fifths thenceforward until he changed again. But in the case of a tenant holding at one-third, no change was made in the rate of batai when the land was changed.

These examples are sufficient to show the great variety there is in batai rents, not only in the same parganah but in the same estate and even village. Moreover the mere rate of batai expresses a very different real share in different villages and to different tenants in the same village as will be seen by comparing Specimen No. 6 with

Specimen No. 8. No hak zemindari was taken from the high caste man.

KANKUT.

Kankut is also a corn rent, but instead of being a division of the actual crop, the outturn is estimated while the crop is on the ground by experts, some short time before it is ripe, but when it has pretty well declared itself. The additions and deductions are made as in batai and in similar variety, but all the calculations are made on the estimated outturn, and the landlord's share alone is weighed out according to the result. There is a money due called 'merhi,' taken to pay for the kut moharrirs at the rate of 5 annas per cent., on the value of the gross estimated produce after deducting the loni. This mode of educing the rent is better than batai, as it removes the temptation to much cheating.

The advantages of corn rents are certainty of collection, and that they do not press hard on the tenants in bad years: their disadvantages are that they afford much opportunity for fraud, require expensive establishments to collect them, throw a large quantity of grain on the landlord's hands when the demand upon him is for money, and encourage slovenly cultivation. Still they are the rents best suited to backward lands or to tracts subject to fluvial action, but they are only suitable as the basis for an assessment when they are taken on the average of a number of years.

SECTION III—MIXED RENTS.

The rents so called by me are really corn rents, though paid in money. They appear to be transition rents adopted on the part of the landlords, because they relieve them of some of the trouble of administering corn-rented lands pure and simple, and by the tenants, because the terms are generally more favorable. There are three kinds known to me in Oudh as already observed.

DARKATTI.

This is the landlord's kankut valued at the harvest price of the threshing-floor after all the adjustments have been made, and is consequently a harvest rent and is payable in money at this valuation. In some parts, however, the landlord gets somewhat more than this by custom. Instead of taking the village prices he calculates at one and sometimes even two panseris less for the rupee, and the darkatti is made on this basis. To give an example, a barley crop is appraised at two maunds for the landlord's share including village expenses, barley selling at one per maund. By the ordinary rule, the rent would be Rs. 2. But suppose the landlord calculates at one panseri less or 35 seers to the rupee, his rent in that case would be Rs. 2-4-6 for his two maunds. If the bazaar rate was very low, he might deduct two panseris and make his calculation at 30 seers the rupee, and in that case he would get Rs. 2-10-8 as his rent. This arrangement prevails in the parganahs farther from the markets, and no doubt is intended to rectify the consequences of a glut in the market at harvest time. In two estates of these parganahs also, which are more inlying and nearer markets, the ordinary custom prevails, with an addition in the one case of three annas in the rupee, and in the other of one to two annas for village expenses.

THAHRAI.

This is also a harvest rent. It is an appraisement of the landlord's share of the crop in money at each harvest, and it is said that on the payment of this sum the tenant is authorized to remove the crop. I suspect, however, that in practice the tenant can hardly pay his rent until he has sold some of his grain and the payment would necessarily be deferred as a general rule. It is stated that where villages are let in lease, this mode of adjusting rent is not uncommon between the lessee and the cultivating tenant in some parts of the Kheri District. It is a fair and sensible mode of procedure, and where they are on friendly terms works well.

Nakshi.

This rent is only found in the Parganahs of Kheri north of the Ul river, and has peculiar features of its own. It is a harvest rent fixed at a money rate per bigah, sometimes on the quality of the soil, but more generally on the time the land has been under cultivation. In the lands where nakshi rents prevail, which are mainly the low lands adjoining the larger rivers, it is customary after cropping the land for several years to abandon it and allow it to recover strength by lying fallow for years together. When the land is again cultivated after this interval, it is termed new land, and pays a lower rate the first year, a higher rate the second year, and the full rate the third. These three rates form the ordinary variations of nakshi rates in the same village. But all nakshi rents vary in reality, if the crop is less than a fair average one, and, as the rates are fixed, it is the area which alters, as will be shown by the following example. Supposing 100 bigahs were cultivated, and the nakshi rate on them was Rs. 2, but at harvest the outturn was found to be that of a three-quarter instead of a full crop, the rate would only be charged on 75 instead of 100 bigahs, and the rent be

Rs. 150 instead of Rs. 200. The true rate of rent in that case is Re. 1-8 and not Rs. 2 a bigah. In the Parganah of Khairigarh, which lies next to Nipál, there is a further custom of deducting an allowance, sometimes *dobiswi* sometimes *chaubiswi*, and known under the name of 'chut.' In other words one-tenth or one-fifth of the cultivated area is never charged with rent at all. To the remainder of the area the nakshi rate is applied, but subject to the rectification at harvest already described. As Khairigarh is peculiarly liable to have its assámis seduced over the frontier by the Nipalese, who offer them all kinds of temptations to settle, the custom of chut has no doubt arisen to counteract these temptations. A native is far more susceptible of a deduction of this kind than if it was given him in the shape of a lower rate of rent.

It will be evident from this description that mixed rents cannot be blindly taken for a single year to make rent rates for purposes of assessment. All three kinds are dependent on the harvest outturn for their figure, and consequently it is only an average of a sufficient number of years that can be relied upon. Moreover, it is necessary besides, in the nakshi rent villages, to add the area struck out at harvest to find the true rent paid in each year, and in the Khairigarh Parganah to include the chut also within that area. Nevertheless, properly and judiciously used, these rents will form the basis of a successful assessment, but it will not be done by going into the villages, inquiring what the rates are, and taking their average to apply to the measured areas of the year of survey.

CHAPTER VI.
PATWARIS AND THEIR PAPERS.

The patwáris of Oudh have been very little interfered with, and as a body they are very incompetent. Their appointment in the first instance rests with the proprietors, and in talukas the Deputy Commissioner is debarred from interference so long as the talukdar furnishes correct papers. This is practically no condition at all, for the patwári is really only required to furnish a jamabandi for money-rented villages. Under present orders, he has no papers to furnish in a grain-rented village. He is supposed besides to maintain a regular day-book and ledger of the village transactions, but there is no adequate machinery to see that it is done. In villages not in talukas, the Deputy Commissioner has to be satisfied of the competence of a patwári on his nomination by the zemindars, and the patwári is supposed to read Hindi fluently, and write it legibly in the Nágri character, to know the simple rules of arithmetic, and to be acquainted with the duties of a patwári as laid down in the Chief Commissioner's orders; but there is no certainty as to either the pay or position of these men, so the District Officers are reluctant to enforce these orders, or rather to try to do so, for it is not at all certain they could enforce them if they tried.

The great obstacle to the reform of the patwári is the existence of the talukdari system as established in Oudh. The talukdars look upon the patwáris as their servants, and they have been encouraged to think so, and they resent any independence on their part. Yet there is no difficulty in showing that the position is both inexpedient and unfair. In corn-rented villages, as the specimens of batai rent divisions will show, the talukdars get one seer in the maund after deducting the allowances for cultivation on account of patwáris, and in money-rented villages they levy, over and above the rent, a half anna in the rupee, or roughly one anna in the rupee on the revenue, a sum larger than the six per cent. which, under the conditions of their kabuliats, they are obliged to pay on this account if the Government chooses to demand it. They do not keep competent patwáris, nor do they pay them regularly and properly. So far for the unfairness of the present system. As to the inexpedience of it, there is little room for doubt. The patwári is the man who is supposed to keep the accounts of both landlord and tenant, and of the lambardars and co-sharers among themselves. There are usually no records whatever beyond his. Under the native system, he was an hereditary officer and himself collected the dues set aside for his remuneration, and he was in a more independent position than he is now; for in the turbulent days of the Nawábi, talukdars were not in a position to coerce their patwáris to the detriment of their tenantry. But now the talukdar has got the Government to consider the patwári his servant; he pays him so far as he is paid; he can get the Deputy Commissioner to dismiss him by a mere request to that effect; and, though I scout the idea of a general falsification of the patwári's accounts, I am not prepared to say that he may not serve his patron in that way in the case of an obnoxious individual, or for a single year to defraud the Government. Rent-suits are decided on the *ipse dixit* of the patwári for the most part, as there is no other evidence forthcoming in nine cases out of ten; for pattas and kabuliats are rare, and there is nothing else but the patwáris' papers. No doubt a ledger supported on the one hand by a jamabandi, and on the other by a regularly kept day-book, is a very trustworthy record; but though this has been prescribed since 1859, and order after order has been issued on the subject, the books are neither generally nor properly kept, partly on account of the inefficiency of the patwáris themselves, and partly because there is not an adequate establishment to supervise them. In my opinion, the patwári should be a local officer supported by the land, perfectly independent of all parties in the village, appointed and dismissed by the Deputy Commissioner, and paid at specified intervals by the tahsildar. There is no objection to a son succeeding his father on condition of fitness, good behaviour, and the punctual submission of the papers, but all three should be rigidly exacted. The patwári is the back-bone of the revenue administration, and besides his payment, independence, and qualification, there are two things further necessary; his charge must be in a ringfence, and he must live in it, and he must keep a gomáshta, so that if one of them be called to court or to the tahsildar, the other may be in his circle attending to its business.

The papers that it is requisite the patwári should keep up in the Province of Oudh, are (1) jamabandi,* (2) roznámcha, (3) báhi kháta, (4) milán khasrah, (5) khewat. It is not necessary to keep up a báhi kháta for corn rents, nor a khewat for a village belonging to one man where there are no under-proprietary holdings in coparcenary, but in such cases the rest, and in all other cases the whole five are required.

---

* In the case of corn-rents this paper is more properly called a *fard batai*, or a *fard kankut*, but there is advantage in using only one word.

In cash-rented villages, the jamabandi is the rent-roll as agreed upon between landlord and tenant, or settled by decrees of court. It is required to show the rent payable by the tenant and is due for the current year, which commences on the 1st July, on the 15th October. I believe however, that the opinion of the courts as to the honesty and independence of the patwáris is shown by their refusing to accept the entry of an enhanced rent in the jamabandi as evidence of the consent of the tenant required by the Rent Act. There is, however, another use of the jamabandi, which is to show what the land actually yielded for purposes of assessment when a new settlement comes to be made, and for this purpose it would be more valuable to show the actual collections than the actual demand. The subjoined form of jamabandi shows both these things, and is as simple as possible. Column 7 would be blank when the paper was filed, and would be filled up from the báhi kháta at the end of the year.

Jamabandi of M—— P—— District—— for 128 F.

1	2	3	4	5	6	7	8
No.	Caste of assámi.	Name of assámi.	Khasrah No. of field.	Area in standard bigahs.	Rent.	Collection.	REMARKS.

Even in cash-rented villages, there are often some few outlying paikásht fields, or fields liable to inundation, which pay corn rents. These it is convenient to have valued in cash by the patwári and entered in the jamabandi. If the village be partly corn-rented, the latter area being considerable, it should have separate jamabandis for each, for reasons that will be apparent when he come to treat of a corn-rented jamabandi. All the jamabandis here suggested are arranged according to the caste of the assámis, because this best shows the differential average of rent. In column 2, however, the zemindars, under-proprietors, or occupancy tenants should be entered separately from the other men of their own caste, being distinguished by the words *sir*, *mátahat*, and *kasthkari* under the caste name, so as to show these particular holdings.

For corn rents, the jamabandi cannot be annual without much compilation, as the rents are harvest rents, the hewant being classed with the kharif as one harvest. As these rents cannot be known until harvest time, to show them in one large form with the cash rents, not only requires a calculation to unite the kharif and rabi, but necessarily delays the cash jamabandi to the end of the year in all villages where both kinds of rent are found. It is quite clear that the patwári must keep a record of each batai and kankut, and if he has to show the whole in one jamabandi, he must compile them, in which much extra labor is involved. Moreover, the people have a great dislike to enter the same land twice in the jammabandi, and consequently when there is a dofasli crop, they only enter the area on which it is grown once in the kharif paper. Yet it is beyond all question that if this area be omitted, the rabi crops will appear to be grown on a much smaller area than is really the case, and both the crop-yield and the crop-rate per acre will be higher than the truth. If the jamabandi be a harvest one, they must enter it, or a crop would appear without an area, which would at once attract attention. On the other hand, the sum of the areas shown in the harvest jamabandis would not be the true total area, and means must be devised to get rid of this

CHAP. VI.] PATWARIS AND THEIR PAPERS.

error, which, however, must be shown to give the true crop-yield and the true crop-rate per acre. This may be done by entering the word 'dofasli' opposite every field in the jamabandi for the rabi in which there was a dofasli crop. It would then be in the power of the compiler to use the extra area or leave it out as he had to show the average yield per acre of any given crop, or the total yield in the year of the land. If there is error either way, there is this difference. In the one case, it is known to the compiling officer, and he can do with it what he pleases, and in the other it is unknown to him and may vitiate all his conclusions. For these reasons, and on the ground of simplicity, accuracy, and ease of supervision, I think corrent jamabandis should be prepared for each harvest, and be due in December and June of each year for the preceding kharif and rabi. The form I suggested should be as follows:—

Jamabandi of M—— P—— District—— for 128 *F.*

1	2	3	4	5	6	7	8	9	10	11	12
Number.	Caste of assámi.	Name of assámi.	Khasrah number of fields.	Area in standard bigahs.	Crop.	Total produce in maunds.	Landlord's nominal share.	Landlord's real share in maunds.	Threshing-floor price per rupee.	Value of landlord's share.	REMARKS.

There is sometimes a difficulty in filling up columns 4, 5, and 7 of this jamabandi where the rents are batai. This is owing to its being the practice of the tenant to put all his grain of one kind into one heap without reference to the field or fields it came from, and then they not only sow utér crops in the same field, but they perhaps sow half a field with one crop and half with another. In these cases, columns 4 and 5 must be left blank, until the system be improved and the grain be threshed and weighed field by field. So with regard to column 7 a glance at the batais given will show that, in some cases, the total produce can only be found by a system of adding together a number of small items in every batai. In Specimens 3, 5, and 6, though the totals are given at the heading of the two former, they really are not known, as the batais commence with a guess that so much is the proper united shares, and they are weighed out accordingly, the balance being eventually divided under the name of kathri after the calculations for deductions have been made. In such cases it would be very laborious to ascertain the total produce, and column 7 would be blank. By improved arrangements generally, however, these difficulties can in time I believe be overcome. In kankut there should be no such difficulty, as I see no reason why the appraisement should not be made even now field by field, and of course it is the total produce that is estimated.

In villages where the rent is darkatti, the second form given will do, if column 10 be headed 'darkat,' and column 11 'rent.' The darkat is sometimes I believe a rate per bigah, and sometimes a price per maund. If the former, the darkat of column 10 will have to be applied to the area, column 5, and if the latter, to the landlord's real share, column 9, to give the rent. Where the rent is thahrai, the second form will also apply, for this, too, is a harvest rent, and as it is usually a rate per bigah, it will appear in column 10 as 'thahrai rate,' and be applied to column 5 to give the rent, column 11.

PATWARIS AND THEIR PAPERS.

For nakshi rents, however, a form of jamabandi peculiar to itself is required. The following I would suggest for this purpose:—

Jamabandi of M—— P—— *District*—— *for* 128 F.

1	2	3	4	5	6	7	8	9	10	11	12
				AREA IN STANDARD BIGAHS.							
					Deduct						
Number.	Caste of assámi.	Name of assámi.	Khasrah number of fields.	Cultivated.	Chut.	At harvest.	Total.	To which rate is applied.	Rate of rent.	Rent.	REMARKS.

The rent is found by multiplying columns 9 and 10, but it is plain, when this form is compared with the description of nakshi rents, that the division of column 11 by column 5 is what gives the true rate of rent for the field. Nakshi lands are, however, as has been already explained, subject to great changes of cultivation, and they pay different rents according as the land is broken up for the first or second year: in the third they pay the full rent. Column 10 of the jamabandi would of itself show which year the field was to be classed in, but, to make it more conspicuous, it is desirable to place the words 'first year' or 'second year' in the column of remarks.

The roznámcha (day-book) is a daily record of every village transaction, and is the source whence the account of each individual is made up. In some shape or other, this record is and must be kept, or the village could not get on; but to make it a really trustworthy record, it should be kept day by day in a bound book, with numbered pages, in which every entry with its date should closely follow the preceding one. The báhi kháta (ledger) requires no remarks, nor does the khewat (register of proprietary mutations) the form of which is found in the Directions.

The melán khasrah is intended to record the annual changes in the cultivation, and it is essential to the proper revenue administration of a village. The form in the Directions is not a convenient one, and I hear it is proposed to substitute for it in the North-Western Provinces an annual khasrah to be prepared by the patwári. This would be an immense improvement, but it is not at all certain that the means for carrying through so ambitious a scheme will be forthcoming. In case they should not, I suggest, as a smaller measure, the following:—

Melán Khasrah of M—— P—— District—— for 128 *F.*

1	2	3	4	5	6	7	8	9	10	11	12
			Cultivation at close of last year.		Fallow during the year.		New cultivation during the year.		Cultivation at close of 128 F.		
Number.	Caste of assámi.	Name of assámi.	Area.	Khasrah number.	Area.	Khasrah number.	Area.	Khasrah number.	Area.	Khasrah number.	REMARKS.

CHAPTER VII.
BOUNDARIES.

THE first work of the Settlement Officer is to see that the boundaries of the mauzahs are distinctly laid down and clearly traceable. This, of course, is a very important duty at the first settlement of a new province, and must not be neglected even at a revision, for boundaries may alter, and partition will, in the mean time, have made separate maháls of lands which it may then be deemed advisable to demarcate into separate mauzahs. The plan followed in Sitapur Division of calling on the people to erect their own boundary marks where there were no disputes, answered well I believe, and certainly saved money to Government.

I wish, however, to put on record that, in my opinion, the man who is selected to make the settlement of a district should do this work. The going over the country engaged in this particular work is simply invaluable to him. He should have ample time to do it, and not be hurried by superior authority; for, while he is doing this work, he should be ascertaining all the particulars mentioned in the preceding chapters, and as he becomes acquainted with them, he will be able to determine and mature the plan on which he proposes to assess the district. He should, at the close of his boundary operations, submit his first report on the assessment, relating in detail his proposed method of working, and if he makes it clear and shows his superiors that he understands what he is about, that they can really follow him as the work progresses, and his proposals appear to offer the prospect of a fair estimate of the gross rental of the lands to be assessed, they should allow him to do his work in his own way. When his report is approved of, the Settlement Officer will be in a position to direct what particulars should be entered in the khasrah. It was a source of great extra cost in Oudh that these entries were made by order of a general circular and without reference to the mode of assessment to be pursued. The required information had subsequently to be added, and men to be sent into every village to do it.

CHAPTER VIII.
SURVEY.

IN Oudh, at the settlement just concluded, there was a double survey, one by the professional department, and the other by the Settlement Officer. I think this was a great waste of power. I can see no reason whatever why the professional department should not furnish a shajrah, khasrah, and list of wells both *kistwár* and *abádi*. Instead then of a second army of amins and munsarims let loose again to plunder the country, there would be but one business of it, and the sadr munsarims, the Settlement Officer, and his Assistant, if he had one, would follow the survey and check the khasrah entries of soils or hárs, cultivation, and irrigation. It appears to me that this arrangement would not only involve less expense, but would ensure the entries being much more carefully made. The settlement establishment would have more leisure to do the testing work, and the fact that their work in part was to be subjected to extra departmental criticism, and possible correction, would put the revenue survey on its mettle. At the same time that the khasrahs were thus tested, the jamabandis could also be tested and the rent rates be made for the assessment. As the khasrahs were tested, they should be sent back to the surveyor who might have a faired out copy of the shajra coloured to show the khasrah entries. The soils or hárs might be indicated by a specifically coloured boundary line, and the cultivators by a distinctive coloured wash for each class, covering the whole field. The irrigated might be distinguished from the unirrigated by a cross mark in the irrigated fields. This coloured copy should be sent to the Settlement Officer as soon as possible, and, in the mean time, the Settlement Officer should submit a report, stating how he found the survey work done, and how he made his rent rates, and submit them for sanction. The khasrah should be nothing but a list of fields. It should have no proprietary columns in Oudh, for in this province entries in it have no signification. The kharif, as well as the hewant, or rabi crop, should be entered opposite each field if it is *dofasli*, and both crops should be entered if it is *utér* as well, for a field may be both dofasli and utér. In the column of remarks should be entered any distinctive classification that the Settlement Officer may have decided upon to make the classification for his assessment. It should also be entered in the column of remarks if the surface of the field is sloping or broken, and whether there be any spontaneous produce in it or not.

CHAPTER IX.
ASSESSMENT.

When the Government has decided the proportion of the rent that is to be taken as revenue, it is the business of the Settlement Officer to determine what that rent may be. A perusal of the previous chapters will show what a number of considerations have to be passed under his review before he can come to any definite conclusions on the subject. At best they can but be approximate, and it is not possible to lay down a precise Code for his guidance. Nevertheless, there are certain rules which, attended to, will greatly assist him in his arduous task. The Settlement Officer, besides finding out what the true rent may be in so far as he can, should also record it in such a form that the demand of the Government assessed at the settlement upon any given piece of land may always be known. To make this record, he must put varying rates on the land classified in some way or other in the settlement papers, and he must show the result in a paper, technically known as the No. II Statement, which is prepared for each mauzah, as the mauzah is the unit of the settlement record. In determining the mode in which he is to arrive at the true rent of the land he has to assess, the powers of the Settlement Officer may have full play, and also in classifying the lands to which he is to apply the rent-rates; and the determination of the rates themselves is a work demanding the greatest care and judgment. The form of the No. II Statement is one of the preliminary points he will have to decide upon, and it is evident that it must vary with his system and be thoroughly adapted to it. In some cases different forms are required in the same district, parganah or even mauzah. To make this statement thoroughly clear to the Commissioner, and that officer should not accept it unless it is so, it must show the incidence of the assessment on the land as classified field by field in the khasrah, and it must give good and sufficient reasons for what is done. It will be plain to any one who reads the chapter on rent, which I am far from thinking exhaustive even for the Province of Oudh, that the same form of No. II Statement is adapted to hardly any two of them. I now proceed to mention the rules that I have referred to and my own experience approves.

I. The Settlement Officer to submit for the approval of the controlling authority a report showing his proposed method of assessment, giving his reasons for adopting it, and forwarding with it a form of No. II Statement such as is suited to his plan. The settlement of the boundary disputes affords the requisite opportunity for collecting the materials for this report.

II. The Settlement Officer to submit a second report showing his parganah rent-rates, and explaining in full detail how he arrived at them. The testing of the khasrahs and jamabandis affords the opportunity for making the necessary inquiries.

III. After the No. II Statements have been prepared as far as they can be before assessment, the Settlement Officer should visit every village with the No. II figures before him, and assess it on those figures, modifying them as may appear to him necessary on his visit, but fully recording his reasons for so doing in the statement. He should declare his assessment at once, and consider and dispose of any objections that may be made on the spot.

These rules may seem rather trite, but they were not observed at the settlement of the province. It may be, and probably would be, that the controlling officers have no more actual settlement experience than the Settlement Officers at a new settlement, for at the end of thirty years the men who made the last one would be gone. But the mere fact of having to explain a system of assessment in detail to the satisfaction of another, ensures that it shall be well thought out, and the controlling officers will have experience in the collection of the revenue and the numerous difficulties that surround it in an unequal settlement, which is experience of first rate value to the work, and is what Settlement Officers who have never been district officers frequently lack.

I would, however, suggest that if the controlling officers find the Settlement Officer's proposals well considered, suitable to the rent systems prevailing in the district, and sensible and reasonable in themselves, they should accept them so far as they conscientiously can. A man will always work out his own ideas with more zeal and success than those of another; and the assistance of experience should rather be given to the Settlement Officer when he is forming his ideas on the subject, when he will receive it gratefully and probably use it to the full; but the work is his, and he should feel that from the first to the last.

The third rule is framed with the double object of enabling the Settlement Officer to have a specific purpose in his detailed final village inspection before assessment, and to enable the Commissioner to follow and check the work in individual villages in detail, and to satisfy himself that the proposals are fair and just both to the malguzars and the Government. We all know the late

Mr. Holt Mackenzie's picture of the observant and receptive Settlement Officer, well versed in the vernacular, gun in hand wandering over the villages, attracting the people by his frankness, and learning from their lips all that was necessary to enable him to assess their lands. This is the very man for the occasion, and the description is perfect of the means towards the enquiry that is to result in the first report. But with reference to the final assessment, it may be laid down as an axiom that unless the sporting Settlement Officer knew in the first instance what he was going to look for, and had some specific object in his inquiries, his rough notes will not be worth much towards enabling him to assess the village, and will be of very little use to the Commissioner. That officer requires a condensed and yet compendious abstract of the basis upon which each mauzah is assessed, with a clear and distinct statement of the reasons why the Settlement Officer sees fit to depart from it in each individual case, and the No. II Statement should show all that.

Although I have stated that the actual system should be left to the Settlement Officer, and that it is not possible to lay down detailed rules which shall be generally applicable, it may not be altogether useless to indicate some of the ways in which an assessment has been and may be made. The general tenor of Section 4 of the Directions to Settlement Officers is vague and oracular, and so far it is good. The warnings in it are sound, and the cautions against over-assessment should be attended to, especially by young officers; for it is an undoubted fact that the greater a man's revenue experience the more urgent he becomes on the subject of the moderation of the assessment, and the less he knows about it the more sanguine are his anticipations of the revenue-yielding powers of the land.

The thing to be ascertained is the rent; not the true economic rent, for the Government has never confined itself to a share of that, but the rent actually paid to the landlord. By landlord is here meant all who share in the rent. There may be in one village a talukdar, an under-proprietor, and a tenant with a right of occupancy, all of whom receive some portion of the rent; and in another village the rent may never be shown in any way in the accounts, because the proprietors are the actual cultivators. But the Government expects the malguzar to pay out of his share of the rent for the patwári and chaukidar, a charge which is estimated at six per cent. on the rental, or twelve per cent. on the revenue, and as these charges are really charges incidental to the cultivation of the land, the rent assessed for revenue purposes is that much above the true rent, and more, because there is the superior management to pay for. It is, therefore, not the economic rent, but the rent actually paid to the landlord that the Settlement Officer has to ascertain. Now, rent is either paid in money or kind, as I have already shown, though under very different circumstances; but, in either case, where there is a rent-receiving landlord, his portion is shown in the village papers. This may not be all the rent, however, and in a coparcenary village cultivated by the proprietors nothing would be shown as rent at all. The accounts of such a village would show how each contributed his share of the revenue, but no *data* from which the rent could be ascertained. But, as a matter of fact, it is not common in Oudh for whole villages to be cultivated by the proprietors. Some there are no doubt, but as a rule even in coparcenary villages, there are some assámiwar rents, and these are usually sufficient to make a village basis for assessment. There are two modes of ascertaining the rent, or the approximate rent paid to the landlord (as I have defined him); the one is to accept the village papers, correcting them for that portion of the rent which is paid to others than the nominal landlord, and the other is to apply arbitrary rent rates fixed by the Settlement Officer to the measured areas of the year of survey.

Of these two modes of arriving at what we must call the assumed rent of the land to be assessed, I myself have far the greater confidence in the former. This system may be applied to all the rents described under the chapter on rent, and if the rents are properly analysed and care is taken in correcting them, the results will give great satisfaction. In adopting this system, it is necessary to remember that though the rates of a single year may be taken where cash rents prevail, it is necessary to make allowances for the average area under cultivation in *sailáb* and paikasht lands, and to be sure that the year is not an extraordinary one as regards the area under cultivation. The people say the *ikbál* of the Sirkár is so great that, whenever a Settlement Officer comes into a district, they are sure to have an extraordinarily good year, and there has been really some foundation for the remark. Where the rents are corn rents, or mixed rents, as I have described them, really founded on the outturn, it is necessary to take an average of years. It is in the parts where these rents prevail also that we find the greatest fluctuations of cultivation. In parganahs where these conditions are present, such as those subject to the action of the Chauka and the Kauriáli, the figures of a single year are as dangerous a basis for the assessment as they are false as a standard of comparison.

The objection made to the first system is that the papers are untrustworthy. This is the language of the Directions to Settlement Officers, and it was the practice of the settlement made under the auspices of the late Mr. Bird so to consider them. But I may be allowed to doubt the fact. I have not found it to be so myself, nor has any other officer whom I know and who has taken the trouble thoroughly to enquire. A jamabandi or a fard batai requires a good deal of sifting and analysis before we can get the true rent of the village out of it, but I firmly believe that, when put through this process, it will give a nearer approximation to the truth than can be reached by any other mode of procedure. I never saw in any of the North-West or the Panjáb Settlement Reports any mention of such sifting or analysis, and I take leave to say that they never got it.*

Under these circumstances, the *dictum* of a high revenue authority that they were worthless may have easily been received as an unquestionable article of faith by his disciples; but until they show me that they have put the jamabandis to the test that I have put them and found them to fail, I decline to accept the *dictum* as fact upon their authority. It is not so easy a matter as some people think for thousands of men to falsify hundreds of thousands of entries with a common object of deceit, when each false entry puts the landlord at the mercy of his tenant both in the matter of paying only the lower rent entered and of exposing the fraud. The only instance of

---

* This alludes to the settlement made under Regulation IX of 1833 not to the recent revisions.

extensive fraud that I have found among village papers has been in villages belonging to Government, and the instigators of it were Government servants acting on the principles of the unjust steward for their own dishonest ends. Even in the case of dolakh, described under batai in the chapter on rent, which prevailed over no great extent of country, they were obliged to keep the true account by the side of the false one. A general coincidence of fraud on such a scale as this is simply impossible, and I prefer to think that those who suspect it do not quite understand the situation.

Though I prefer an assessment based on the village papers, I do not mean to say that a successful assessment may not be made upon arbitrary rent rates fixed by the Settlement Officer and applied to the classified areas of a single year, where the rent system admits of fixing the rates from tolerably reliable *data*. This system is, however, not suited to lands the cultivation of which varies from year to year, especially when the newly broken-up land pays a lower but increasing rent. It may answer where true money rents are found with a sufficient number of rates to suit the classification of the soils, but the rates being average are apt to be low on the best and high on the worst lands, and to press hard on the poorer class of villages. It is true that the Settlement Officer is not expected blindly to adhere to his rates, but where they are far out an unnecessary responsibility is thrown upon him when he visits the village, and he is set a task very hard to perform with any degree of self-reliance. All the assessments that have had to be revised in Oudh have been made on this principle, and the general story is the same, " the jama was too heavy on the poor lands."

As to what are called test jamas, which are calculations of so much per head of cultivating assámis, so much per plough, so much per homestead, and so on, I have no faith in them. There is no possible comparison between the outturn of a Kurmi and a Thákur family off so many acres of similar land, nor of their ploughs either. One officer showed me five such jamas which he had worked out for a parganah which he had assessed at about a lakh, and the difference between the highest and the lowest was Rs. 40,000. In individual villages it would probably be even proportionally greater, and such tests can be of no practical use whatever, though they may serve as pegs whereon to hang a general disquisition on the subject of the assessment in the Settlement Report. If a controlling officer is to see that the assessment is really a good one, he must carefully study, appreciate, and correct the reports mentioned in Rules I and II, and finally himself examine and be satisfied with the No. II. Statements of each particular village. If his charge be too great to enable him to make that final examination, he can be satisfied with the Commissioner's reasons for his approval, and await the test of time to a certain extent before he signifies his sanction to the assessment.

Although I disclaim being able to suggest any method of assessment which will meet all cases, and I think it best that, under general supervision, each Settlement Officer should devise his own, yet, to show how assessments based upon dissimilar elements have been and can be made, the most convenient way will be to give one or two specimen No. II Statements, and to explain how they are to be filled in. I have, therefore attached five different forms of No. II Statement. Of these, four are suited to assessments based on the village papers, and one to assessments based on arbitrary rent-rates applied to the areas of the year of survey. I now proceed to describe them one by one.

The form No. I is intended for a village where the rents are money-rents fixed and ordinary. The principle of this system is to analyse the rents, so that the differences between them may be very clearly shown, and to correct those rents which seem to require it. The upper part of the statement is general information about the village, and is the same in all the five forms except the classification of the soil, which, of course, may vary as the soils and as the Settlement Officer may desire to show them. In the "detail for assessment," the classes of holdings speak for themselves. Nos. 1, 2, 3, and 4 usually pay less than the full rent of the land, though Brahmins often pay full or nearly full rents. No. 5 always pay exceptionally high rents. No. 6, as a rule, pay the fair average rents, and they form the standard of assessment. Sometimes the rents shown under No. 6 'others' will evidently not be true rents. In such case the Settlement Officer must make a special inquiry regarding them, and he will always find the cause. The zemindari class may be among the 'others' or the talukdar may pay a mutsaddi or a patwári in low rented land, for example; such lands must be eliminated, and the true average rate will then appear. The soil classification is that determined by the Settlement Officer, and recorded in the upper part of the statement. In the specimen given it is by hárs. The area is that of the khasrah survey, and the rent that of the jamabandi. The division of the rent by the area gives the rate. The result is that the Settlement officer can see at a glance the comparative rate of rent paid by the different holders for similarly classified land. The rent-free land is shown separately, and the soil column is filled up with the suitable Roman numeral corresponding with the classification of the soil. It may be that under-proprietary rent-free land may be of more than one quality, and in that case as many classes of soil must be allowed as are necessary, a line being added for each; but generally these holdings in single villages are small, and one classification will do. Máafi means small revenue-free grants; belagán* rent-free lands granted by the proprietor and resumable by him; charri grazing land; and chakarána service lands rent-free, such as the chaukidar's holding when he is so paid. Máafi, groves, and Charri would not be assessed; but the other three are under existing rules liable to assessment. The area column would be filled in from the khasrah survey figures. The remarks on rent-free tenures should explain anything unusual about them, and the reason for not assessing them when exempted. So far as possible the paper should be filled in before the Settlement Officer visits the village, all in fact except the columns under 'proposed,' the 'rate,' and 'total' of the rent-free lands, and the remarks on both sides of the paper.

In order that the Settlement Officer may compare the lands similarly classified, but bearing different rates of rent, the shajrah should be coloured. In this case the outside of the goind or inlying manured land might be indicated by a red line, and the outside of the manjahár or intermediate land by a green one, and similar lines might

---

* This word is also used in parts of the Kheri district, to signify cultivated land, the crops on which have been destroyed by wild beasts or by hail or frost, and on which no rent is paid.

be drawn indicating the locality of each classified soil according to the system adopted. Each kind of holding should be indicated by a separate coloured wash over the whole field. In this way with* the No. 2 statement and the shajrah before him on the back of an elephant, the Settlement Officer can go over the village and look at any of the lands which he pleases, knowing exactly the comparative rate of rent it pays. After such an inspection, he can have no difficulty in filling up the rate column under 'proposed' with proper rates representing the value of the land according to the fair village assámiwar rates, or so much less than that as in his judgment would suit the case of a thákur or a zemindar. These rates applied to the khasrah areas will give approximately the real rent-roll of the village. To this would be added what he put upon the rent-free land, as after examining it he would have to enter a rate in the rate column of rent-free, and also whatever might be assessed on the cultivable waste that was productive. By this I mean the spontaneous growth or yield which can be sold for money on the spot, what that would fetch should be the measure of the value of the land. Half the sum of these three would give the jama, and the cesses should be added at $2\frac{1}{2}$ per cent.

Form No. II is intended for a village where there are special money rates for certain crops, alternating with money or corn rents. The classification of the soil is different from the last one and is merely specimen. The only remark perhaps required is to explain 'bijar.' This is a word used in the east of Oudh to signify a cold clayey soil in which rice is the main crop, though sometimes when the rice is not transplanted, a crop of grain is taken off it in the spring. Under the head "area and rental for ten years," the figures are entered from the village papers, and the rates are deduced by dividing the rents by the areas. In all three the areas are the jamabandi areas, and the rents of the zabti and nijkari are the rents actually paid. Under 'batai,' the rent column is to be filled up with the value of the landlord's share of the produce, as finally arranged, at the village threshing-floor price of the harvest. The rates would be worked out in the usual way. The result of this would be an average rent-roll of the village which might be depended upon for assessing the land to the revenue. But this is not enough. The assessment has to be recorded so as to show its incidence on any given bigah of land which this alone would not do, and consequently the form contains a table headed "assessment on classified soils." The area here is the khasrah area, and the rates those fixed by the Settlement Officer from what he finds existing. In these cases, the rents must be average, for the land that is zabti one year is nijkári or batai the next, and the kachiána land under zabti rent pays very different rates as the crop may be vegetables, tobacco, or potatoes. Hence the Settlement Officer, with a distribution of this kind before him, would probably find it best to put only nijkári and batai lands into the areas of the classified soils, and make a common rate for them in each class, noting the fact below, so that if any zabti lands should be carried away by diluvium, a special allowance may be made. In this case the shajrah should be coloured according to the soils as classified, and marks should show the fields that are zabti in the year of survey.

The assessment here should be on the average of the ten or other number of years that may be selected. If the papers of ten can be got, it is a fair average, and with a proper system for the patwáris and their papers there should be no difficulty about it at a new settlement. Hence the Settlement Officer should, under the head 'proposed,' show rates which will give a jama approximating to that of the average ten years' rental. His village inspection with rates and coloured shajrah before him would enable him to do this. Should it prove difficult to arrange the rates on account of a great difference of area shown in the total by the khasrah and the average of the jamabandis, the total of the khasrah should be compared with the jamabandi result of the year of survey, and if they agree it will prove that the area under cultivation is too fluctuating for the figures of a single year to be used, and the average area should be entered under the column for area "at fixed rent rates." If they do not agree but differ considerably for the year of survey, the presumption would be that the village papers were not correct, and a thorough enquiry into them would naturally follow. Should they correspond, however, and the average classified rents have to be entered, they will be found in the manner described in the next case. The rent-free lands are in addition, as they are not included either in the average area or in the khasrah area at fixed rates, and the assessment put upon them would have to be added whichever areas were used.

Form No. III differs but slightly from Form No. II. The classification of the soil is simpler and suited to lands which have no permanent system of irrigation. Under "detail for assessment" five years only are given, but that is on account of space merely. They would be better to be ten. Under the head of 'kankut,' the estimate of the crop in grain will be valued at the threshing-floor prices. Indeed there is no distinction between it and darkatti as far as the valuation is concerned, and the headings are only shown separately that it may be manifest how much rent is paid in money and how much in kind. The reason why under "at fixed rent rates" an average of five years was put as well as the year of survey, is explained in the last para. It is actually entered in this form, because the classification shows a village more liable to a fluctuating cultivation. The classified area of the five years' average would be found from the melán khasrah, a paper which it is absolutely necessary to keep up in estates the cultivation of which fluctuates greatly, and which should be arranged to show the changes in cultivation according to the settlement classification of the soil. The rates it would be the business of the Settlement Officer to determine, and I shall make some remarks on this hereafter.

Form No. IV is for nakshi rents, and as the rate of rent is one-third the first year of cultivation, two-thirds the second year, and full rates thereafter until the land is abandoned, it is clear that we must show the land under these three rates separately. In the chapter on rents under 'nakshi' the system is explained. Here it will suffice to say that column 8 is (column 2 − column 7), and that column 9 is (column 3 × column 8), while column 10 is (column 2 ÷ column 9). The nominal rent column 4 is (column 2 × column 3) and is inserted to show how far out would be a settlement, where these rents prevail, based on the cash rates in the parganah papers. The area of the classified soils for assessment must be average areas where nakshi rents prevail, but they should be the average of each class cultivated, without deductions. The true rates should be found by the deductions in each class and then be applied to the average area of each under cultivation.

Form No. V is that suitable to an assessment by arbitrary rent rates on the areas of survey. I have enlarged it somewhat and shown the rent-free land separately, though that is not strictly the system. Officers assessing on this system generally divide their villages into first, second, and third class, and even a fourth class sometimes. In the first case with the classified soils given here, they would have 18, and in the second 24 rates in the parganah, that is, six in each class of villages. The best assessments that I have seen made on this system have been where a number of rates were used. Where only a few were used, the assessments proved unequal, being brought up by over-assessment of the poorer lands. I have already said that this system can be applied where the rents are suited to it. These rents are ordinary money rents. Fixed rents would always be assessed at full rates under this system, for they are not distinguished, and I think, as a rule, they cannot bear as high an assessment as assámiwar rents. But even with money rents in this case, as in the case of Form No. I which is also based on the areas of a single year, care must be taken that it is not a year with an abnormal area under cultivation. I have seen an assessment where corn-rents prevail successfully made under this system, but only by one officer who described his system of making rent-rates, and the general opinion on his assessment is that it is low.

In fixing the rent rates, the Settlement Officer must be

guided by his own intelligence and the materials that he finds to hand. Where ordinary money rents prevail, a careful estimate of those paid on the several classified lands in a certain number of truly average villages is what will have to be made, and he must trust to his own personal judgment alone to make the necessary alterations in the column headed 'proposed.' Where corn rents prevail, it must be carefully remembered that the money rents found side by side are special rents, and are no true basis from which to deduce rent-rates for the purpose of assessing corn-rented lands. Assuredly assessments based on rates derived from such a source will fail. The only sure way to make rent-rates for corn-rented lands is as follows: 1st, to make a most careful selection of average lands from which to deduce them; 2nd, to find the rent by applying to a careful estimate of the actual produce the threshing-floor price of the grain forming the landord's share after making all the customary deductions and additions; 3rdly, to divide the rent thus found by the classified area on which the crop was grown; 4thly, to find the average rates given by the above operation for a series of years. This system of finding rent-rates for corn lands is on the face of it very laborious, and it is rendered still more hard to accomplish on account of the difficulty of identifying the classified soil on which the crop is grown. A Settlement Officer may select the classified soils and have the crops on them cut in his presence and their value determined on the spot, but he can only do this in one year, and that will not suffice; for, not only is the yield of a single year a fallacious basis to go upon, but the rotation of crops brings more valuable and less valuable produce into the account in different years and thus vitiates the calculations. No doubt well devised and carefully prepared jamabandis would give the data, but we have not yet reached that revenue consummation. The Board of Revenue, North Western Provinces, has, I believe, prescribed an annual khasrah, which, if they can get it, will solve these difficulties. The rates are difficult to be arrived at under a reliable system, and, as a matter of fact, are generally reached in a much rougher way.

At page 110 I have alluded to one officer who successfully assessed lands paying corn rents by fixed rates of rent. The following extract shows how he arrived at them. The rates to be found were for manjahár (intermediate) lands. "On taking twelve or twenty acres from amongst "the middle hár of nine villages, chosen from all parts of "the parganah by random and not design, I found that "the outturn of grain on those paid as rent, converted into "cash at the price current calculated at *harvest prices* of "the five years preceding survey, gave the following "results: On taking the average of the whole on irrigated "land Rs. 4-9-7, and on unirrigated land Rs. 2-14-0, giving "revenue rates of Rs. 2-5-0 and 1-7-0 respectively. The "fields thus chosen, it must be remembered, were picked "from the maps at random, and not from selected villages "but from villages of all sorts, and in fixing therefore on "Rs. 2-8-0 for villages of the first class, and Rs. 2-4-0 and "Rs. 2 for those in the second and third classes for irrigat-"ed lands, with Re. 1-12, Re. 1-8, and Re. 1-4 for unirri-"gated, I do not think I was otherwise than on the safe "side."

This is the most careful and systematic way of making rent-rates in corn-rented lands which has actually come under my observation, and the result was a successful assessment though generally low, yet it does not come up to the requirements of the last para. but one. The fields are not carefully selected average ones but taken at random; although the prices are a five years average, the produce is that of one year alone, and it may be out as an average year both in the yield and on account of the particular crop that happens to be grown that year; and three rates for first, second, and third class villages are assumed from a basis which at best is supposed to be the average of all.

As regards the deduction of rent-rates from the other cash rents, it will be plain that zabti rates can only be applied to lands cultivated under that system or rather to the average area of such land for a series of years. Katti is a true money rent as far as it goes, but, if found side by side with zabti, to deduce the rates from the katti alone would be to give away Government revenue: each would, therefore, have to be applied to its own area, either for one year or an average of several as the proportions of land rented under the different systems was fixed or variable. The same remarks apply to nijkári, which is always side by side with zabti rents. Darkatti, thahrai, and nakshi, being all dependent on the outturn, can only be used to give rent-rates by taking the average of several years.

All the forms of No. II Statement attached to this volume have the result of parganah or chak rent rates shown when applied to the classified area. In form No. I this is shown for purposes of comparison alone, but in Nos. II, III, and IV, columns headed 'proposed' are added to it, and they are intended to show the rates which have to be applied to the classified soil to make the total equal to the jama assessed, which is avowedly not based on the parganah rates. These proposed rates are however necessary, for without them the district officer would not know the jama assessed on any given bigah of land, and, unless such knowledge be forthcoming, I affirm that the settlement record is not worth the name. To all five forms the village inspection is a common mode of correcting the results, but No. V has to depend on this to a very much greater degree, because there is no other check upon the average rent rates, as it proceeds on the erroneous assumption that the village papers are necessarily incorrect. With all the five forms, however, a shajrah, coloured to suit each or any of the classifications that may be adopted, will be found of invaluable assistance at the personal inspection of the village.

These forms I repeat are merely specimen, but they are improved by my own experience from models which have been more or less actually in use. I think that all No. II Statements should contain what these do, the indication of the system of assessment that is to be pursued. The prescription of a single form for all villages as is done in the Directions is a mistake, and that form is not a good one for any kind of village that I know. The information contained in a No. II Statement should all conduce towards one end, and not be a collection of isolated facts bearing every relation to one another if combined, but so presented that no use can be made of them for the common end of rational assessment. No single form should be prescribed at all. Two or more may be advisable in the same parganah and even in the same village. They should in all cases be drawn in harmony with the system of rent which prevails in the lands they are to be applied to, and they will themselves then indicate what must be prepared to fill them up and to assess the land revenue in that particular village. In these remarks I have taken no notice of the old system of assessing large areas by rent rates and subsequently distributing the jamas over the villages included in such areas. In the old time the first part was done by the Settlement Officer, and the second by his native assistants. It tied the latter down to make the total square with the parganah figures of the former, and is a system altogether so inferior to the assessment village by village that I fancy it is now-a-days everywhere abandoned.

There remains one question which I can barely avoid discussing here, and that is whether fifty per cent. is too much for the Government to take as land revenue. In the Decennial Settlement of Bengal, Behar, and Orissa in 1789, which was afterwards made the Permanent Settlement of 1793, the Government took ten-elevenths of the estimated rental. This was followed by a very extensive change in the *personel* of the proprietors of the land in that province, so great that in many parts none of the old families have been left. But in other places the estimate of the rental was very imperfect, and where that was low and the proprietors managed to scrape through the earlier years of the Permanent Settlement, the advancement of the country made the assessment fall lightly on them, and they are now very well off. This is also the case with the capitalists who succeeded the old sold-up zemindars buying the estates at auction. The estates that were permanently over-assessed from the first have fallen into the hands of the Government by the operation of the sale law and the absence of bidders, and these estates are managed by the Collectors under the name of khásmaháls, and are mostly farmed on account of Government. Though this Permanent Settlement has been eminently successful in so far that it has created a class of wealthy landed-proprietors in Bengal, it is very doubtful whether the advantages which have flowed from it are such as to embrace any other class of the community, while it is certain that the measure has alienated from the Government a large and unexceptional source of increased revenue; and the greatest revenue authorities of the present day doubt the wisdom of the Bengal Permanent Settlement at the time, and are satisfied that it is not a measure to be imitated in other parts of India.

In the North-Western Provinces at the settlement of 1833, the Government nominally took 66 per cent. of the estimated rental. This, however, did not leave to the proprietors 34 per cent. for themselves as there was a charge besides for the patwári and chaukidar which the zemindars had to pay, and which was subsequently estimated at 6 per cent. on the rental, and a charge of 1 per cent. on the demand, or $\frac{2}{3}$ per cent. on the rental, for district roads. The total charge on the zemindars therefore was $72\frac{2}{3}$ per cent. leaving the people $27\frac{1}{3}$ per cent. for their share. Under this assessment, which was levied on a much more careful estimate of the rental than that of the Decennial Settlement in Bengal, Colonel Baird Smith's Report showed conclusively that the general prosperity of the North-Western Provinces had advanced in a very marked degree. Nevertheless, the Revenue Authorities came to the conclusion that it was too high: the system of collection was rigid, and though estates were not sold for arrears of revenue, they were sold in large numbers in execution of civil decrees for debts incurred to pay up the revenue; and about 1854, the Saharunpur Settlement instructions were issued fixing 50 per cent. of the estimated rental as the Government demand. These instructions also fixed the mode of estimating the cesses, which placed half the charge for chaukidar, roads, schools, and district dâk upon the Government share. This, including the patwári whose salary was charged entirely against the zemindar, made the total demand $55\frac{7}{8}$ per cent. But at the recent revision of settlements in the North-Western Provinces, the principle of charging the cesses according to the Saharunpur instructions was abandoned, and it was laid down that the zemindars were to pay the whole, and the total demand including the patwári is now 58 per cent. In Oudh the like system prevails, and there, including the local cess rate, the total charge is $58\frac{1}{2}$ per cent. In these calculations, the chaukidar and patwári are each estimated at 3 per cent. on the rental.

As a matter of fairness I think that the road and school cesses ought to be paid by the zemindars entirely, and, on the other hand, the Government ought to pay half the salaries of the chaukidars and patwáris as they are as much public as village servants. If the chaukidar is paid by a chakarána rent-free holding, it should be exempted from assessment. The district dâk should be a charge on the Post Office which exacts postage on the letters delivered through it, and the Oudh margin fund might be given up. This then, including the local rate cess in Oudh, would make a total demand from the zemindar of $55\frac{1}{4}$ per cent.

I think that $55\frac{1}{4}$ per cent. of the rental is not more than an ordinary talukdar or zemindar can pay to the Government. I am of opinion, however, that where there are large under-proprietary interests in an estate and these under-proprietary rights are much sub-divided, and even in villages held direct from Government by high caste men forming a numerous community, so large a percentage should not be demanded. I think that discretion should be allowed to officers making a settlement to reduce the percentage of the Government demand in such cases. It is impossible to say to what limit, for it depends entirely on circumstances, and it must be left to the superior revenue officers to check any undue tendency in the direction of making the percentage too low. To me this appears a far more honest course than declaring the assets less than they are really known to be.

But I am speaking of Oudh, where a first regular settlement has just been made. What was taken at Annexation was a summary assessment which was sanctioned only for three years, and the people knew all along that their payments were to be revised as soon as the Government could do it. Generally speaking, therefore, it might be considered fair and not impolitic to insist on the real half rental assessment as a starting point. Yet it has been found necessary in many cases, and it is now admitted as part of the policy of the Oudh Government, to allow the assessment to increase by annual increasements up to the half rental assessment where the rise was sudden and large. When we come to make a new assessment at the end of thirty years of a fixed demand, we should be warned by what has recently occurred in the North-Western Provinces. Even where the demand has not exceeded what the Government was entitled to, after thirty years of our rule and of fixed demand, there has been a great outcry against the revision where the increase has been considerable. Native landholders live up to their income, and they cannot meet an enhanced demand all of a sudden:

they are thrown into difficulties as soon as they try to meet it.

I think that, while the land should be assessed on its actual rental at the time of making the assessment, in revising one of our own assessments at the end of thirty years, we should not at once take the result of such assessment, but rather add to the demand in each year, so that we shall have reached the full assessment at the end of the new period of thirty years, instead of at the beginning. Probably thirty years is too long a period for this operation, and twenty years would be a better time at the end of which to make a fresh estimate and begin a new rise if the increased rental justified it. The probability is that this slow and gradual but steady rise, all of which would be known beforehand and covered by the actual rental, would operate as a gentle but practical stimulus to agricultural improvement, while the Government would feel that the land ought to be well ahead of the revenue demand upon it. As after a revised assessment the same process of a gradual increase in the demand would be continued, there would not be anything like the same temptation to falsify the village papers, and if they were properly attended to on their submission, and testing enforced as was recommended by Mr. Holt Mackenzie so far back as 1822, though not yet attained in the North-Western Provinces (*vide* Sir John Strachey's Review of the Board's Report 1872-3), there would be no occasion for a re-survey of the land at the time of a new assessment. A No. II Statement drawn up from the jamabandi of the last year of a true money rented village, or from the average of ten years' actual collections, if the rents were corn or mixed, would, when compared with the No. II Statement of the previous assessment, enable the district officer, after a personal inspection of the village, to assess the land. In holding this view of the matter, I believe that I am in very respectable company, and I think that, if some such system is not adopted, and we continue to demand the full rise at once on the occasion of each revision of assessment, the Government will find itself compelled on every such occasion to reduce the proportion of the revenue demand, as it has twice done already on this side of India, has done I believe in Madras, and is now doing in Bombay. It is only an annual progressive increase within the limit that can keep up the proportion of the revenue to the rent in the face of the increasing population of rural India. Gradually so applied, it may induce the people to turn to other industrial pursuits or diminish their number by emigration, but sudden rises under such circumstances must produce discontent if not riot and rebellion.

CHAPTER X.

COLLECTION OF THE REVENUE.

WHEN I first drew up the plan of this little book, I intended to confine my remarks under this head to the collection of the revenue strictly, presuming the rent to be collected for the purposes of this chapter. The collection of the rent by the landlord and the revenue by the State are, however, so intimately connected, that, on further consideration, it appeared to me that to suppose the rent to be collected would look so like begging what many would call the main issue, that I feel I must say a few words on the subject of rent collection.

In order that he may pay his revenue, the landlord must collect his rent where he is not also the cultivator, and he has to do this from three classes of persons, tenants-at-will, occupancy tenants, and under-proprietors. This is done under a law of procedure called the Rent Act of which there is one to each Government. The Oudh Rent Act is generally admitted to be effective for this purpose, as regards the two first classes, if it receives two main amendments. These are—1st, to make the procedure for the distraint of the standing crop more prompt and effectual; 2nd, to protect the tenant by a clause that when the landlord receives a remission of revenue on account of some calamity beyond his control, the tenant shall receive a proportional remission of his rent. It is, however, absolutely necessary that in this latter case the relief should be given at once; and in Oudh the great difficulty which is experienced in making such relief prompt arises from the miserably inadequate establishment allowed for the collection of the revenue in that province.

In the collection of rent from the under-proprietors, however, other and great difficulties arise. No power of distraint nor of summary ejectment is allowed by law. The landlord has first to get a decree which he does without difficulty, and he has then to execute it which practically he cannot do at all, or if he can, it is after such delay as seriously to embarrass his own affairs, and to throw the revenue into arrears. He is not allowed to proceed against the tenure, until he has exhausted processes against the moveable property, of which there is never any to be found, and when allowed to attach the tenure he is not allowed to sell, until after direct management has been tried. The Court has the power to appoint the landlord manager, but this is rarely done, and then the Court can invest him with no more power over the under-proprietor, after perhaps years of delay, than the landlord possessed in regard to tenants from the first. If the Deputy Commissioner be appointed manager, he is armed with all the powers he has for collecting the revenue, but the Deputy Commissioners have far too much to do already, and so this resource is seldom adopted.

In this difficulty, and it is a very serious one, I think that if we turn to the old native rules, they will help us. No man has any right to hold land paying revenue to Government, unless he pays the rent which may be due upon it, and if he defaults, the remedy must be sharp and prompt, or it is no remedy at all. I propose that an improved procedure of distraint be made applicable to the holdings of under-proprietors as well as to those of tenants to meet the case of an under-proprietor cultivating his own land; and that, in addition, if the landlord has got a decree for arrears of rent, and such decree remains unsatisfied for one month, he should be authorized summarily to eject the under-proprietor, on the condition that, if the latter pays up the arrear without interest, he shall be entitled to be reinstated at the commencement of the next ensuing agricultural year after he makes the payment. This will meet the case of the rent-receiving under-proprietor.

Of course there are holes as wide as a barn-door to be picked in such a proposition as this. It may be said that it is unfair, because the profits of an under-proprietary holding are generally far more than the fair interest of the rent of it for a single year, and that at least the landlord ought to account for them. It may be said that it is unfair to the new tenant to eject him at any time, merely because the old defaulter has scraped the money together and has reappeared upon the scene. Or it might be that the under-proprietor could not collect his rents or gather his crop from the vicissitudes of the season, and a hard landlord or karindah, who wished to get rid of him, might urge on so prompt a procedure as this to his utter ruin. Or it might be said that where the under-proprietors were in cultivating occupancy of the whole of the land or nearly the whole of it, were numerous, and contumacious, the measure could not be carried out and would fail. Nevertheless, as a general measure, it would be acceptable to the people and would not fail. The landlord would like it, because he would see the way to the regular realization of this rent, and the under-proprietor, because his connection with the land would not be severed for ever, as it is by our procedure when all its cumbrous forms are gone through. There would be hope where there is no hope, and a motive for exertion which does not now exist.

But I must examine the objections mentioned *seriatim*. In the first place the management of a defaulting estate of this description is not the costless thing some people imagine, and the profits of the landlord would probably not be so very outrageous, while it is strictly in accordance with the manners and customs of the people and has its almost exact counterpart in the simple usufructuary mortgage. To demand an account from the landlord would be to spoil the whole scheme. It would lead to fraudulent papers on the one hand, and frivolous objections to the accounts on the other, interest would become an element, for in such case it must be allowed, and the Courts would be flooded with litigation. I cannot myself see the hardship of it when compared with our revenue legislation. We transfer a patti entirely until the pattidar pays up the arrear, and, if so, why not an under-proprietary right? It would be hard to make a villager see the difference. As to the new tenant, he would seldom be the victim of such a measure, as in about one-half of the cases he would remain the old tenant, the under-proprietor not being in cultivating occupancy, and in cases where the under-proprietor was in cultivating occupancy, I apprehend a ready system of distraint would be more commonly adopted as the means to get the rent paid. But when a new tenant succeeded a cultivating under-proprietor, he would know exactly the nature of his tenure, and if he recognized any real disability in it, he could stipulate to pay only such rent as would make it worth his while to take the land. Any complaints from him at his ejectment from such a cause would not meet with the village sympathies, and I think he may be safely left to those of his condolers. But, should legislative sympathy with him prove to be greater than that of his co-villagers, a fairly long term of limitation might be laid down within which the ejected under-proprietor might redeem his holding.

As to the plea that the rent or the crop could not be got in on account of floods, hail, frost, drought, &c., the tenant might be allowed to plead that in the suit for arrears of rent, and the Court (who would usually be the Tehsildar and know all about it), if a *primâ facie* case was made out, should stay proceedings and report to the Revenue Authorities, and, on their certifying that it was a case for a remission of revenue, the Court might decree the arrears less a deduction proportionate to the remission. It is not in such cases that the landlords are hard on their people as a rule.

The last case I honestly confess my proposal does not meet, nor does any other that I ever heard of. It is a case in which the villages as at present constituted cannot and will not pay half of the gross rental calculated at rates paid by ordinary cultivators. They are high caste men, they occupy all the land, they simply squat there and wont pay, and they would probably commit a riot if not allowed to remove their crops, while no one dare take their land if they were ejected. The cases of such villages are however not numerous, and they must be specially dealt with by the Government, either by such a reduction of the jama as will enable them to go on as before, or by providing some other mode of subsistence for the people. No law common to all will ever deal with such exceptional cases.

For the collection of the revenue as distinct from the rent, it appears to me that two measures of improvement are required in Oudh, the one having reference to its collection in co-parcenary villages holding direct from Government where the proprietary body is numerous and holds much of the area in its own cultivation, the other to the case of villages held wholly or partially in under-proprietary tenure, in which the under-proprietors have paid their rent, but the proprietor has not paid his revenue. The remedies that I shall propose to meet these cases, though different from the nature of the problems they deal with, rest on the same principle, that the real individual defaulter shall be made responsible as completely and thoroughly as possible.

In dealing with a co-parcenary proprietary body, the rule is that the Government shall deal with the lambardar, and Section 101 of the Oudh Rent Act enacts that in a joint estate he alone of the coparceners can exercise the powers of that Act for the recovery of rent and other purposes : this also applies to under-proprietary communities. Generally speaking, this rule works well enough, but when there are quarrels between the lambardar and his co-sharers, it does not work, and particularly where the co-sharers are very numerous in the east of Oudh. If the co-sharer cultivates the land himself, he pays nothing to the lambardar, unless the latter has great force of character, and the tahsildar has to set aside the malguzari register altogether and collect from each individual coparcener, if he wants to get in his revenue at all; and, even when there are tenants under a numerous coparcenary, the coparceners frequently collect from the assámis the rents of their separate, and their share of the rent of the joint lands, and the tahsildar has to collect individually all the same. It is no use fulminating against this state of things : it is one of those facts which don't square with our rules but which we must face and deal with nevertheless. I would simply recognize it, abolish Section 101 of the Rent Act altogether, and allow the tahsildar to proceed against the land in a man's several possession whether there had been a regular partition or not. It is useless to tell them to apply for a partition, for they wont do so in the first place, and it takes many months to make one in the second. Such villages would become hopelessly involved before the partition could be effected, and besides the full partition is neither desired nor required.

But it is to the law for the cancelment of settlement previous to sequestration or sale, as it affects under-proprietors who have paid their rent, that I wish to draw attention. It cancels the settlement of the defaulter and all underproprietary rights created by him, but it does not cancel under-proprietary rights recorded at the settlement. To me this law appears as unjust as it is inexpedient. Why should one of these men have his tenure confiscated for ever in case of sale, and for any time up to fifteen years in case of sequestration and direct management, and the other be exempted from all responsibility, though both are settled on the same land which had not paid its revenue to Government? Why indeed? Both have paid their rent and both have been created by the same man, but the one happened a few days before the Settlement Officer made the record of that village and the other a few days later. What is there in this that should make this tremendous difference in the way of treating these two men? As to the expediency of the law, it is enough to say that, as long as it lasts, it is impossible to do justice to those holding underproprietary rights in an estate which defaults in the payment of its revenue: if it be possible, let those who say so show it, I for one do not know how.

It is an incident of under-proprietary tenure that it is liable for the revenue in the last resort whether the rent on it has been paid or not, and the revenue law should always be drawn with reference to this principle. If this is to be the guide, it is plain that the cancelment should extend to the whole settlement, whether there be decrees for the under-proprietary tenures or not, and then there must be a new arrangement based upon the rights and liabilities of the parties before the Government and among themselves. This new arrangement should, in my opinion, take the form of a temporary settlement in case of sequestration, and the term of the sequestration should not only be determined as a punishment to the defaulter, but also with a view to carry out the principle above mentioned. With this object, as the Government has a right to its revenue, it may be necessary temporarily to increase the rent of an under-proprietor, so that the arrears may be collected in a reasonable time; but in justice, the temporary settlement should provide for, and the term of the sequestration should be extended until the under-proprietor has been repaid, with interest, out of the share of the proprietor, all the extra rent he has been made to pay on the latter's account.

When a settlement is cancelled with a view to the sale of an estate for arrears of revenue, all the under-proprietary rights should be also cancelled whether secured by decrees of Court or not. Should there have been under-proprietary rights in the estate, their nature and extent should be inquired into, and if held at rents lower than the Government revenue assessed upon the land, extra land should be given out of the estate until the profits of the under-proprietors, when charged with the full revenue assessed by the Government, equal those which they formerly enjoyed under a lower rate of rent. The remainder of the property should then be sold; and, if it covered the arrears as in nineteen cases out of twenty it would, and as it ought to do if the Deputy Commissioner knows his business, a direct settlement might be made with the former under-proprietors, and their lands become new mahals. If the arrears were not covered by the sale of the land left after making these new estates, the balance should be recovered from the former under-proprietors, under the orders of the revenue authorities as may seem fair and equitable. It is impossible to say in proportion to their holdings, or indeed to lay down any hard and fast rule, for a proprietor just before breaking up might alienate his lands to his relatives or friends for the purpose of fraud. On the other hand, the protection of those under-proprietary rights recorded at settlement alone may be very unjust, as the defaulting proprietor may have received the full value for those subsequently created, and the protected may hold under a legal but very less equitable title.

In this matter the Government may safely rely on the discretion of their revenue officers on the spot controlled by their official superiors. Justice would be done, and the people would show no misgivings.

In this short chapter I have not attempted to speak of the general mode of collecting the revenue, which is explained in the Directions far more lucidly than I can do it. I have confined myself to remarks on those points in the collection in Oudh for which the Directions do not seem to provide, or where the Oudh Rent Act can be shown to be inadequate or cumbrous in procedure.

TALUKDARI
Hadbast No.   Mauzah

Area.	Bighas.	No.	Classified S
Cultivated		I	Kachiána
Cultivable, productive ...		II	Bijar
„ not productive ...		III	Domat, irri.
Sites ...		IV	„ unirri.
Roads ...		V	Bhur, irri.
Tanks		VI	„ unirri.
Groves			
Nalas and ravines ...			Assámis
Barren ...			Chapparband ...
			Paikasht ...

DETAIL

Area an

Year.	Zabti.			N	
	Area.	Rent.	Rate.	Area.	R
1281 F. ...					
1282 „ ...					
1283 „ ...					
1284 „ ...					
1285 „ ...					
1286 „ ...					
1287 „ ...					
1288 „ ...					
1289 „ ...					
1290 „ ...					

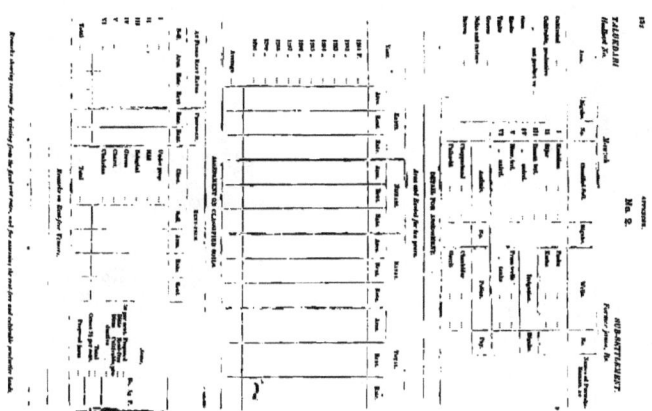

APPENDIX.

No. 2.

SUB-SETTLEMENT.
Former jama, Rs.

oil.	Bigahs.	Wells.		No.	Names of Purwahs, Bazaars, &c.
...	...	Packa	...	...	
...	...	Kacha	...	...	
...	...	Irrigation.		Bigahs.	
...	...				
...	...	From wells	...	...	
...	...	„ tanks	...	...	
	No.	Police.		Pay.	
	...	Chaukidar	...	...	
	...	Gorcit	...	...	

FOR ASSESSMENT.

l Rental for ten years.

KARI.		BATAI.			TOTAL.		
ent.	Rate.	Area.	Rent.	Rate.	Area.	Rent.	Rate.

TALUKDARI
Hudbust No.   *Mauzah*

Area.	Bigahs.	No.	Classified S
Cultivated		I	Kachiána
Cultivable productive ...		II	Clayey soil
,, not productive ...		III	Sandy soil ...
Sites			
Roads			Assámis
Tanks			Chapparband ...
Groves		•	Paikasht
Nalas and ravines ...			
Barren			

DETAI

FIRST YEAR OF CULTIV

Years.	Area cultivated.	Rate.	Nominal Rent.	ARE. Chut.
1281 F. ...				
1282 ,, ...				
1283 ,, ...				
1284 ,, ...				
1285 ,, ...				

SECOND YEAR OF CULTIVA

1281 F. ...				
1282 ,, ...				
1283				

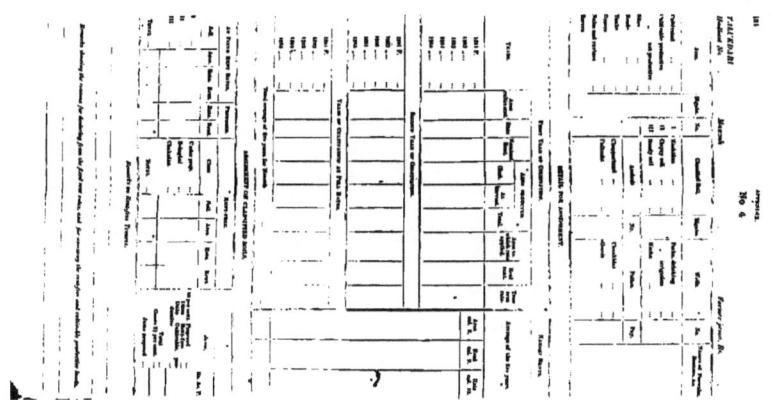

APPENDIX.

No. 4.

Former jama, Rs.

oil.	Bigahs.	Wells.		No.	Names of Purwahs, Bazaars, &c.
...		Packa, drinking	...		
...		„ irrigation	...		
...		Kacha ...	...		
	No.	Police.		Pay.	
	...	Chaukidar	...	...	
	...	Goreit ...	...	...	

L FOR ASSESSMENT.

ATION.					NAKSHI RENTS.		
DEDUCTED.		Area to which rate applied.	Real rent.	True rent rate.	Average of the five years.		
At harvest.	Total.				Area col. 2.	Rent col. 9.	Rate col. 10.
TION.							

APPENDIX.
No. 5.

FIRST CLASS VILLAGE.　　　　　　　　　　　　　　　　　　　　**PATTIDARI**

Hudbust No. . 　　*Mauzah* . 　　*Former jama, Rs.*

Area.	Bigahs.	No.	Classified Soil.	Bigahs.	Wells.	No.	Names of Purwahs, Bazaars, &c.
Cultivated ...	...	I	Goind ...	...	Pucka ...	...	
Cultivable, productive	...	II	Bijar...	...	Kucha ...	...	
,, not productive	...	III	Doamat, irri. ...	...	Irrigation.	Bigahs.	
Sites ...	...	IV	,, unirri. ...	...			
Roads	...	V	Dhur, irri.	...	From wells	...	
Tanks	...	VI	,, unirri. ...	...	,, tanks ...	...	
Groves	...						
Nalas and ravines	...		Assamis.	No.	Police.	Pay	
Barren ...	...		Chapparband ...	...	Chaukidar ...	...	
			Paikasht ...	...	Gorait ...	...	

DETAIL FOR ASSESSMENT.

At Fixed Rent Rates.				Proposed.		Rent-free.				
Soil.	Area.	Rate.	Rent	Rate.	Rent.	Class.	Soil.	Area.	Rate.	Rent.
I	...					Under prop.	...			
II	...					Muā̃fi ...				
III						Belagāni	...			
IV						Groves ...	...			
V	...					Charri ...				
VI	...					Chakrána	...			
Total ...						Total ...				

Remarks on Rent-free Tenures.

Jama.　　　　　　　　　　　Rs. As. P.
50 per cent. Rent-paying ... ...
Ditto　Rent-free ... ...
Ditto　Cultivable, productive ...
　　　　　　　　　　　Total ... ...

Cesses 2½ per cent. ... ...

Proposed jama ...

Remarks showing the reasons for deviating from the fixed rates, and for assessing the rent-free and cultivable productive land.